Free Will: A Very Short Introduction

VERY SHORT INTRODUCTIONS are for anyone wanting a stimulating and accessible way in to a new subject. They are written by experts, and have been published in more than 25 languages worldwide.

The series began in 1995, and now represents a wide variety of topics in history, philosophy, religion, science, and the humanities. Over the next few years it will grow to a library of around 200 volumes – a Very Short Introduction to everything from ancient Egypt and Indian philosophy to conceptual art and cosmology.

Very Short Introductions available now:

ANCIENT PHILOSOPHY
  Julia Annas
THE ANGLO-SAXON AGE
  John Blair
ANIMAL RIGHTS   David DeGrazia
ARCHAEOLOGY   Paul Bahn
ARCHITECTURE
  Andrew Ballantyne
ARISTOTLE   Jonathan Barnes
ART HISTORY   Dana Arnold
ART THEORY   Cynthia Freeland
THE HISTORY OF
  ASTRONOMY   Michael Hoskin
ATHEISM   Julian Baggini
AUGUSTINE   Henry Chadwick
BARTHES   Jonathan Culler
THE BIBLE   John Riches
BRITISH POLITICS
  Anthony Wright
BUDDHA   Michael Carrithers
BUDDHISM   Damien Keown
CAPITALISM   James Fulcher
THE CELTS   Barry Cunliffe
CHOICE THEORY
  Michael Allingham
CHRISTIAN ART   Beth Williamson
CLASSICS   Mary Beard and
  John Henderson
CLAUSEWITZ   Michael Howard
THE COLD WAR
  Robert McMahon

CONTINENTAL PHILOSOPHY
  Simon Critchley
COSMOLOGY   Peter Coles
CRYPTOGRAPHY
  Fred Piper and Sean Murphy
DADA AND SURREALISM
  David Hopkins
DARWIN   Jonathan Howard
DEMOCRACY   Bernard Crick
DESCARTES   Tom Sorell
DRUGS   Leslie Iversen
THE EARTH   Martin Redfern
EGYPTIAN MYTH
  Geraldine Pinch
EIGHTEENTH-CENTURY
  BRITAIN   Paul Langford
THE ELEMENTS   Philip Ball
EMOTION   Dylan Evans
EMPIRE   Stephen Howe
ENGELS   Terrell Carver
ETHICS   Simon Blackburn
THE EUROPEAN UNION
  John Pinder
EVOLUTION
  Brian and Deborah Charlesworth
FASCISM   Kevin Passmore
FREE WILL   Thomas Pink
THE FRENCH REVOLUTION
  William Doyle
FREUD   Anthony Storr
GALILEO   Stillman Drake

GANDHI Bhikhu Parekh
GLOBALIZATION Manfred Steger
HEGEL Peter Singer
HEIDEGGER Michael Inwood
HINDUISM Kim Knott
HISTORY John H. Arnold
HOBBES Richard Tuck
HUME A. J. Ayer
IDEOLOGY Michael Freeden
INDIAN PHILOSOPHY
  Sue Hamilton
INTELLIGENCE Ian J. Deary
ISLAM Malise Ruthven
JUDAISM Norman Solomon
JUNG Anthony Stevens
KANT Roger Scruton
KIERKEGAARD Patrick Gardiner
THE KORAN Michael Cook
LINGUISTICS Peter Matthews
LITERARY THEORY
  Jonathan Culler
LOCKE John Dunn
LOGIC Graham Priest
MACHIAVELLI Quentin Skinner
MARX Peter Singer
MATHEMATICS Timothy Gowers
MEDIEVAL BRITAIN
  John Gillingham and
  Ralph A. Griffiths
MODERN IRELAND Senia Pašeta
MOLECULES Philip Ball
MUSIC Nicholas Cook
NIETZSCHE Michael Tanner
NINETEENTH-CENTURY
  BRITAIN Christopher Harvie and
  H. C. G. Matthew
NORTHERN IRELAND
  Marc Mulholland
PARTICLE PHYSICS Frank Close
PAUL E. P. Sanders
PHILOSOPHY Edward Craig
PHILOSOPHY OF SCIENCE
  Samir Okasha
PLATO Julia Annas
POLITICS Kenneth Minogue
POLITICAL PHILOSOPHY
  David Miller
POSTCOLONIALISM
  Robert Young
POSTMODERNISM
  Christopher Butler
POSTSTRUCTURALISM
  Catherine Belsey
PREHISTORY Chris Gosden
PRESOCRATIC PHILOSOPHY
  Catherine Osborne
PSYCHOLOGY Gillian Butler and
  Freda McManus
QUANTUM THEORY
  John Polkinghorne
ROMAN BRITAIN Peter Salway
ROUSSEAU Robert Wokler
RUSSELL A. C. Grayling
RUSSIAN LITERATURE
  Catriona Kelly
THE RUSSIAN REVOLUTION
  S. A. Smith
SCHIZOPHRENIA
  Chris Frith and Eve Johnstone
SCHOPENHAUER
  Christopher Janaway
SHAKESPEARE Germaine Greer
SOCIAL AND CULTURAL
  ANTHROPOLOGY
  John Monaghan and Peter Just
SOCIOLOGY Steve Bruce
SOCRATES C. C. W. Taylor
SPINOZA Roger Scruton
STUART BRITAIN John Morrill
TERRORISM Charles Townshend
THEOLOGY David F. Ford
THE TUDORS John Guy
TWENTIETH-CENTURY
  BRITAIN Kenneth O. Morgan
WITTGENSTEIN A. C. Grayling
WORLD MUSIC Philip Bohlman

Available soon:

AFRICAN HISTORY
  John Parker and Richard Rathbone
ANCIENT EGYPT Ian Shaw
THE BRAIN Michael O'Shea
BUDDHIST ETHICS
  Damien Keown
CHAOS Leonard Smith
CHRISTIANITY Linda Woodhead
CITIZENSHIP Richard Bellamy
CLASSICAL ARCHITECTURE
  Robert Tavernor
CLONING Arlene Judith Klotzko
CONTEMPORARY ART
  Julian Stallabrass
THE CRUSADES
  Christopher Tyerman
DERRIDA Simon Glendinning
DESIGN John Heskett
DINOSAURS David Norman
DREAMING J. Allan Hobson
ECONOMICS Partha Dasgupta
EXISTENTIALISM Thomas Flynn
THE FIRST WORLD WAR
  Michael Howard
FUNDAMENTALISM
  Malise Ruthven
HABERMAS Gordon Finlayson
HIEROGLYPHS Penelope Wilson

HIROSHIMA B. R. Tomlinson
HUMAN EVOLUTION
  Bernard Wood
INTERNATIONAL RELATIONS
  Paul Wilkinson
JAZZ Brian Morton
MANDELA Tom Lodge
MEDICAL ETHICS
  Tony Hope
THE MIND Martin Davies
MYTH Robert Segal
NATIONALISM Steven Grosby
PERCEPTION Richard Gregory
PHILOSOPHY OF RELIGION
  Jack Copeland and Diane Proudfoot
PHOTOGRAPHY
  Steve Edwards
THE RAJ Denis Judd
THE RENAISSANCE
  Jerry Brotton
RENAISSANCE ART
  Geraldine Johnson
SARTRE Christina Howells
THE SPANISH CIVIL WAR
  Helen Graham
TRAGEDY Adrian Poole
THE TWENTIETH CENTURY
  Martin Conway

For more information visit our web site
www.oup.co.uk/vsi

Thomas Pink

FREE WILL

A Very Short Introduction

OXFORD
UNIVERSITY PRESS

OXFORD
UNIVERSITY PRESS

Great Clarendon Street, Oxford OX2 6DP

Oxford University Press is a department of the University of Oxford.
It furthers the University's objective of excellence in research, scholarship,
and education by publishing worldwide in

Oxford New York

Auckland Bangkok Buenos Aires Cape Town Chennai
Dar es Salaam Delhi Hong Kong Istanbul Karachi Kolkata
Kuala Lumpur Madrid Melbourne Mexico City Mumbai Nairobi
São Paulo Shanghai Taipei Tokyo Toronto

Oxford is a registered trade mark of Oxford University Press
in the UK and in certain other countries

Published in the United States
by Oxford University Press Inc., New York

© Thomas Pink, 2004

British Library Cataloguing in Publication Data

Data available

Library of Congress Cataloging in Publication Data

Data available

ISBN 0–19–285358–9

1 3 5 7 9 10 8 6 4 2

Typeset by RefineCatch Ltd, Bungay, Suffolk
Printed in Great Britain by
TJ International Ltd., Padstow, Cornwall

Foreword

The free will problem is an old one. Like anything old, it has changed over time. This book has three aims, therefore: to introduce the free will problem as it exists now; to explain how the problem has come to take its present form; and to suggest how the problem in its present form might be solved.

This book is meant to provide not merely an introduction, but also an original contribution to its subject. The views presented here are developed at greater length in other books and articles that I am in the course of publishing. The relevant references are to be found at the end in the section of Further Reading.

My thanks to Tim Crane, Peter Goldie, Jennifer Hornsby, Tim Norman, and Martin Stone, to an OUP reader, and to my wife Judy. Each has read the text of this book in its entirety, and made many very helpful suggestions.

T.P.
London, New Year's Eve, 2003

Contents

List of illustrations x

1 The free will problem 1

2 Freedom as free will 22

3 Reason 43

4 Nature 55

5 Morality without freedom? 73

6 Scepticism about libertarian freedom 80

7 Self-determination and the will 91

8 Freedom and its place in nature 104

References 124

Further reading 125

Index 130

List of illustrations

1 David Hume, by Louis
   Carrogis   12
   © Scottish National Portrait
   Gallery

2 St Thomas Aquinas,
   woodcut of 1493   30
   © 2004 TopFoto.co.uk

3 Duns Scotus   32
   © Scottish National Portrait
   Gallery

4 Thomas Hobbes, *c.*1669–
   70, by J. M. Wright   57
   By courtesy of the National
   Portrait Gallery

5 John Calvin, *c.*1550,
   French School   77
   Museum Boÿmans Van
   Beuningen, Rotterdam

6 Immanuel Kant, 1791,
   by Dobler   101
   © 2004 TopFoto.co.uk

Chapter 1
The free will problem

What is the free will problem?

Some things are firmly outside your control. What has already happened at times in the past before your birth, what kind of universe you live in – these things are in no way up to you. Just as much outside your control are many features of your own self – that you are human and will die, the colour of your eyes, what experience is now leading you to believe about your immediate surroundings, even many of the desires and the feelings that you are now having.

But there are other things that you do control. These are your own present and future actions. Whether you spend the next few hours reading at home or going to the cinema; where you go on holiday this year; whether and how you vote in the next election; whether you stay working in an office or leave to attempt writing as a career – these are things you do control. And you control them because they consist in or depend on your own deliberate actions – actions that are up to you to perform or not. As a normal, mentally healthy adult, how you yourself act is not something that events in nature, or other people, just impose on you. Where your own actions are concerned, you can be in charge.

This idea of being in control of how we act – the up-to-us-ness of our actions – is an idea we all share. It is a constant and fundamental feature of our thinking, and one that we can all recognize. And the idea is irresistible. However sceptical we may become when doing philosophy, once we fall back into ordinary life we do all continue to think of how we act as being up to us. Thinking of ourselves as being in control of how we act is part of what enables us to see living as something so valuable. In so far as we can direct and control how we ourselves act, our lives can be genuinely our own achievement or failure. Our lives can be our own, not merely to be enjoyed or endured, but for ourselves to direct and make.

Or so we think. But are we really in charge of our actions? Is how we act truly up to us as things such as the past, the nature of the universe, even many of our own beliefs and feelings, are not? The problem of whether we are ever in control of how we act, and what this control involves, is what philosophers call the free will problem.

And a problem it is. No matter how familiar the idea of being in control of our actions might appear, there is nothing straightforward about it. Whether we have control over how we act, and what this control requires and involves, and whether and why it matters that we have it – this is one of the very oldest and hardest problems in philosophy.

The long history of the free will problem shows up in its name. *Freedom* and *will* are two words that we in everyday life do not ordinarily much use when talking about our control over, the up-to-us-ness of, our own actions. Nevertheless for the last 2,000 years or more Western philosophers have used precisely these terms to discuss this problem of whether we really do have control over how we act. Their choice of these words *freedom* and *will* tells us something about why it might matter whether we do have action control – and what this control over how we act might involve. Let me say something about each word, starting with *freedom*.

The Greek philosopher Aristotle discussed actions and our control over them in one of the oldest and most important discussions of morality by a philosopher – the *Nicomachean Ethics*. But in the *Ethics* though Aristotle talked of us as having control of how we act – he stated that our actions are *eph hemin*, or, literally, 'up to us' – he did not actually use *eleutheria*, the Greek word for freedom, to describe this action control. *Eleutheria* was still a term used only in political discussion as a name for political freedom or liberty. It was in the period after Aristotle that Greek philosophers began using *eleutheria* in a new and entirely non-political sense, to pick out the idea of being in control of how we act. And ever since then philosophers discussing the up-to-us-ness of our actions have followed the later Greeks: the same term *freedom*, which is used to pick out political liberty, has also been used to pick out an individual person's control over their own actions. If what you do really is within your control, then you can be said to be *free* to act otherwise than as you actually are doing. You are, as philosophers put it, a *free agent*.

So we have two uses of the term *freedom* – to refer to political liberty and to refer to our action control. And these two uses are importantly different. For enjoying political liberty is one thing – but having control of how you act is quite another. Political liberty has to do with our relation to the state, and so too to a wider community of people of which we form a part. In particular, political liberty has centrally to do with how far the state avoids restricting the activities of its citizens through laws and legal coercion, whereas action control is nothing directly to do with any such relation to the state. Someone could be a free agent – have control over their own actions – even when they lived quite alone on a desert island, outside any political community, and so where there could be no issue of their enjoying or lacking political liberty. But even though enjoying political liberty and being in control of how one acts are not the same, the history of theorizing about action control has been full of analogies with the political, and this is no accident. It is in fact quite natural that one and the same term should be used to pick out our control over how we act and a fundamental political value.

There is, after all, a certain analogy between action control and political liberty. Having some degree of control over our lives gives us a certain independence within nature – an independence that sticks and stones, and perhaps even the lower animals, do not have. We are not dictated to and driven by nature, but stand within the universe rather as citizens do within a free government or state – a state that allows its citizens a measure of political liberty, and in particular some share in the determination of what happens to them. Like a free state, nature too leaves a part at least of our lives to us to direct. Nature, too, grants us a measure of liberty.

But this analogy is not the end of the story – though it may have especially weighed with the ancient Greek philosophers, many of whom, particularly the Stoics, the school of philosophers who named themselves after the *stoa* or colonnade in Athens where they originally met to discuss and teach, did see nature as something of a cosmic state, a state governed and ruled by reason. More important for us today, I suggest, is the fact that having action control, being a free agent in this sense, has a clear political significance – a significance for freedom considered as political liberty. For there is a plausible link between our status as people who enjoy control over how we act and the value to us of liberty in relation to the state. If we could not or did not think of ourselves as capable of controlling our own lives, as capable of being in charge of our own destinies, then surely political liberty – the state allowing us to direct our own lives and destinies in the political sphere – would not be recognizable to us as an important value. So why not use the same term to pick out both our action control and the political value that seems to depend on that action control?

What of the term *will*? This term has been used by philosophers in a variety of ways. But one especially important use has been to pick out a vital psychological capacity that all normal adult humans possess – a capacity for decision-making. We are all capable, not only of performing actions such as going to the cinema or staying home and the like, but of first deciding for ourselves about which such actions to perform. This capacity to make decisions or choices seems central to our capacity to control and take charge of our own actions. Indeed, we commonly convey the 'up-to-us-ness' of our actions by referring to their connection with our own decisions. 'It's up to me what I do! It's my decision!' people insist.

Freedom of action may even depend on a freedom specifically of decision-making – on a freedom of will. It may be up to us how we act only because we have a capacity for deciding how we shall act, and it is up to us which such decisions we take. This is more or less what I shall be arguing – and what many philosophers once believed. But since the 17th century, philosophers within the English-language tradition – philosophers working in Britain and America – have often denied that freedom of action has anything at all to do with freedom of will. Whatever we might ordinarily think, they claim, there is no such thing as a freedom of decision-making, or at any rate our freedom of action is entirely independent of it. Behind this dispute about the will and its relevance to freedom is a deep dispute about the nature of human action.

Our freedom, we must remember, is a freedom of action – a freedom to do things or to refrain from doing them. By contrast, freedom is not, at least immediately, a characteristic of non-doings. Take wants and desires, or take feelings. Wants and feelings are clearly not actions. Considered in themselves, they are just states that come over us, or which we find ourselves with. Wants and feelings or sensations are passive in the sense of being things that happen to us, rather than being things that immediately arise as our own deliberate doing. And because wants and feelings are not actions, because they are passive happenings to us, wants and feelings lie outside our immediate control. It is not directly up to us what we want or feel, as it is up to us what actions we perform.

Sometimes, of course, what we want or feel is within our control. But that is only ever true because we can, to a degree, influence what we want or feel through our prior actions. I can, for example, increase my desire for food by taking a run; or I can reduce pain by applying ointment, or by deliberately concentrating my mind on last year's holiday, and so forth. My direct control of my actions can, through the effect of my actions on passive occurrences such as wants and feelings, give me some indirect control over these wants and feelings as well. Our control over our actions extends to give us control over those actions' consequences too. But our freedom is still ultimately a freedom of action. Freedom is always exercised through action – through what we deliberately do or refrain from doing – and through action alone.

This tight connection between freedom and action is very important. It means that to understand what freedom involves, we shall also need to understand the nature of human action, that medium through which, it seems, we can exercise our freedom.

Here we come to the issue of decision-making and its place in freedom. Especially in late antiquity and in the Middle Ages, philosophers used to explain the link between action and freedom in terms of the will. The very term 'free will problem' as a description of a problem about freedom of action reminds us how general was this belief in an identity of freedom of action with freedom of will. Freedom was taken to be essentially a characteristic of decision or choice – all freedom was a freedom of the will. We immediately controlled our decisions – and we controlled everything else through our decisions. Freedom was tied to action because decision-making or choice was a central component of, indeed the immediate form taken by, human action. Freedom applied to action, then, because to act was to exercise a free will.

Were philosophers ever right to believe in this will-based theory of action? Were they right to believe in an identity of freedom of action with freedom of will? As we shall see, there are important objections to their theory. And certainly, more recent English-language philosophy has tended to suppose that this will-based theory of action and freedom was a mistake. In fact, modern philosophy in Britain and America has often gone to the opposite extreme. It has tried to claim that action and control of how we act really have nothing whatsoever to do with the will or with any freedom of the will. But this modern reaction, I shall be arguing, is also an error. If we try entirely to detach action and our control of it from the will and its freedom, then, rather than understanding freedom better, we shall end up disbelieving in it entirely. To take the will out of the free will problem is, in effect, to take away the freedom as well.

Without the will, we shall be unable to make sense of freedom of action at all. We shall end up thinking, as do many modern philosophers, that the whole idea of our actions being free and up to us is just a confusion. And that is precisely what many modern philosophers do think; not merely that, as a matter of fact, we happen to lack control over how we act (as if things could have been different), but that freedom of action is something impossible – something that necessarily no one could ever possess, because the very idea of it is muddle and contradiction. Belief in freedom of action, modern philosophical fashion has increasingly come to suppose, is an incoherent delusion – as incoherent as belief in a round square.

Freedom and morality

But before we consider in more detail why our freedom of action could be such a problem, we need to look further at the significance of freedom – at why it might matter whether or not we are free. We need to look at the place of freedom in morality. And here, again, the spotlight is on action.

We naturally think that action – what we ourselves do or refrain from doing – has a special moral significance. A vital part of ordinary morality centres on individual moral responsibility – on the idea that people can be accountable for how they live their lives. Now what we are immediately responsible for in our lives is our action. We are each accountable for what we do and fail to do. Or so we ordinarily suppose. If, for no good reason, you have deliberately acted in a way that you knew would hurt or harm someone else – perhaps you deliberately made a wounding comment to a friend – you can be to blame for the hurt you have caused. Others will certainly blame you and hold you responsible; and as you come to think about what you did, you may well come to blame yourself too. You may come to feel guilt for what you have done.

Morality presents us with standards that are obligatory, that we are responsible for keeping to, and that we can rightly and fairly be blamed for not meeting. And these standards apply to action. The same burden of responsibility does not lie on feelings or desires – at least those feelings or desires that come over us independently of our own doing. I may, for example, experience a feeling of hostility towards you; but if this feeling just came over me – if the feeling was not the result of anything I had done, and if there was nothing I could have done to prevent it – how can I be to blame for it?

We are to blame for what we ourselves do or fail to do; but not for what happens to us independently of our own doing. This view of responsibility is very natural and familiar. But what makes moral responsibility something that we have for how we act and for the consequences of how we act, but not for anything else?

Key to any plausible explanation must be a link between moral responsibility and some form or other of *self-determination*. It is of the essence of blame – the holding someone responsible for committing a wrong – that it is targeted on the agent himself. We are, after all, asserting that it is the agent himself – that very person, and not merely some event or process connected with him – who is responsible. What we are holding the agent responsible for must therefore be something that can properly and fairly be identified with and put down to him. What we are holding the agent responsible for must be something that he determined for himself would happen. It must be something determined by the agent's very own self – something self-determined as we might say. If we are morally responsible for our actions, but not for our feelings and desires, the explanation why must be that the relevant kind of self-determination may be found in action, but is not to be found in desire or sensation.

Common sense, it seems, has a clear explanation for why we are morally responsible for our actions but not, say, for our feelings and desires. Common sense appeals to freedom – to what we control or to what is up to us. It is directly up to us how we act – but not what feelings we have or what desires come over us. We have action control, but no direct, action-independent feeling or desire control. That is why we are morally responsible for our actions, and not for our feelings and desires.

This appeal to freedom to explain moral responsibility is very natural; and that is because the exercise of control or freedom is the most immediately intuitive form of self-determination. We naturally identify the agent with the exercise of his freedom. It is the agent, after all, who is in control.

The idea of being a free agent – of being in control of how we act – seems, then, to lie at the heart of our moral thinking. Reactions of blame and guilt are only fair if, in doing what you did, how you were acting really was within your control. It must really have been up to you whether you made that wounding comment or not. If your making the comment was wholly outside your control, how could you be to blame for the fact that you made it?

If it is our freedom that supports and justifies emotions such as blame and guilt, then human freedom is also presupposed in our legal systems, when courts punish people and hold them legally to account for what they have done. For punishment counts as genuine punishment, as opposed to mere constraint or violence, only if it is imposed on wrongdoing as something that is supposed to deserve the punishment. Punishment has built into it the claim that the person punished really was to blame for doing wrong – and so that they really were responsible for doing what they did. But then punishment is fair only if the person punished was in control of their actions – if it really was up to them whether or not to act as they did.

Not all our actions need be within our control. Perhaps someone might be a genuine kleptomaniac, gripped by a compulsive desire to steal – a desire that takes away their freedom not to steal and literally compels them to take things. If this is possible, then their stealing could perfectly well still be a genuine action of theirs – something they deliberately did. But lacking the freedom not to steal, their action would not be something for which they were responsible. If the key notion for moral responsibility is freedom, action is our responsibility only in so far as it really is free – something really within our control to perform or not.

This view that moral responsibility depends on freedom may be very natural. But it is also very controversial. Many philosophers would deny that what I have presented as the common-sense view really is or should be common sense. In modern philosophy there is absolutely no agreement about whether freedom matters in morality – or even that action has any special moral significance. One important reason for this disagreement is simple. Freedom of action has proved so puzzling an idea – to the point nowadays of often being thought incoherent and impossible – that philosophers have become increasingly inclined just to ignore or abandon the notion when doing moral philosophy. They have tried to make sense of morality without talking about freedom.

Some philosophers would still accept that we are morally

responsible for our actions, and for our actions alone. But they would deny that this responsibility depends on our actions being free. There is some other feature of action, something that is nothing to do with our having control over it, that makes us responsible for how we act. Or perhaps they take our peculiar responsibility for our actions as something that does not need explanation.

But other philosophers have been even more radical. For the 18th-century Scottish philosopher David Hume, morality was not at all about being responsible for what we do. In his view, we do not have a special moral responsibility for our actions – a responsibility that we lack for those of our characteristics that are not our doing. Actions are not what really matters in morality; they are at best effects and signs or symptoms of what really matters. Morality is more about desire and emotion – about the passive states of motivation, feeling, and character that precede our actions and cause us to perform them – than it is about actions themselves. Morality is primarily about being an admirable and virtuous kind of person. Performing the right actions – doing the right thing – is something secondary, something that merely follows on and results from being a virtuous person.

Can we understand morality and moral responsibility without appeal to freedom? I shall be arguing that we cannot. Action really does have a special importance in morality. We really are responsible for what we ourselves do, as we are not for what just happens to us. This special responsibility for our actions does need explaining, though. And, as we shall see, what explains this special significance that action has can only be freedom. Once we understand what human action really involves, and in particular once we understand the role played in human action by the will, we shall see that no other explanation of our moral responsibility for our actions will work. Putting the will back into the free will problem means putting our freedom and how we exercise it back into the heart of morality.

1. David Hume, by Louis Carrogis

But why so much disbelief in freedom? Let us now turn to what threatens our freedom of action – to precisely why the free will problem is a problem.

Why we might not be free

Most of us start off by making an important assumption about freedom. Our freedom of action, we naturally tend to assume, must be incompatible with our actions being determined or necessitated to happen by prior causes outside our control. Suppose, for example, that by the time of your birth, the world already contained causes – be they the environment into which you were born or the genes you were born with – that determined exactly what throughout your life you were going to do. Then at no stage could how you act possibly remain up to you. If, from the very beginning, it has all along been determined exactly how you must act, how could you possibly be free to act otherwise?

Causal determinism is the claim that everything that happens, including our own actions, has already been causally determined to occur. Everything that happens results from earlier causes – causes that determine their effects by ensuring that these effects must occur, leaving no chance for things to happen otherwise. So if causal determinism is true, then at any time what will happen in the future is already entirely fixed and determined by the past. And we naturally think that the truth of causal determinism would definitely remove our freedom. Our natural assumption is that our having control of how we act depends on our actions not being causally determined in advance by factors outside our control – by factors such as the environment we were born into, the genes we were born with, the desires and feelings that come over us beyond our control. This assumption that we so naturally make is called *Incompatibilism*, so-called because it says that freedom is incompatible with the causal predetermination of how we act by factors outside our control. We are natural incompatibilists.

But that is not all that we are. We are natural libertarians too. *Libertarianism* about freedom of action combines Incompatibilism with the further belief that we do actually possess control over how we act. Libertarians are incompatibilists who believe that we really are free. And that is exactly what we naturally suppose. Though we think the predetermination of our actions would remove our control over whether we perform them or not, we still strongly incline to suppose that we do possess that control – that it is we who are in charge of how we act, and that past causes are not imposing our actions on us. Libertarianism, and so too Incompatibilism with it, is our natural theory of freedom.

The intuition that Incompatibilism is true – that our freedom of action depends on our actions not being determined in advance – is very general. For most people who are new to philosophy, nothing else makes any sense. The very possibility that when they were born their every action was already predetermined and fixed – this they see as a very clear and obvious threat to their freedom. People coming to philosophy for the first time are very reluctant to give Incompatibilism up. But Incompatibilism presents us with deep difficulties. In fact Incompatibilism promises to make freedom something impossible. Or so many modern philosophers suppose.

The threat of determinism

The first difficulty is obvious. Incompatibilism places an important condition on our freedom of action – the absence of causal predetermination by conditions outside our control. But can we actually know that this condition is met? We do not normally think of how we act as already determined by past causes. Yet how can we be sure? Perhaps, after all, causal determinism really is true. Perhaps everything that happens in the universe is determined to occur by prior causes. In which case, by the time of our birth, our every action will already have been causally determined in advance.

The belief in causal determinism – that the world is a deterministic system – was defended, in the ancient world, by the Stoics. Belief in causal determinism became common again among Western philosophers after the 17th century. And this was because the new forms of science then being developed, and in particular the physics of Newton, provided us with deterministic laws that appeared to explain and govern the motion of every physical object within the universe. Incompatibilism left the up-to-us-ness of our actions, with all that morally depends on it, pitted against what then seemed an all-too-plausible world picture – the picture of the world as a deterministic physical system suggested by 18th- and 19th-century science.

Since then the plausibility of causal determinism has lessened. Twentieth-century physics left universal determinism a very much less well-supported picture. For, on certain interpretations of modern quantum physics, the world is indeterministic at the level of the very small. The motions of small sub-atomic particles, at least, lack determining causes. As undetermined the motions of these small particles are, to some degree at least, *chancy* or *random*.

Of course our actions occur at the level of the visibly large, not the invisibly small – at the macroscopic level, not the microscopic. And might that not still leave some threat from determinism? Perhaps we do not know with any certainty how far indeterminism holds for such macroscopic events. Even if there is some microscopic indeterminism, much variation in what happens at this microscopic level may make no difference to what happens at the level of the large. In which case microscopic indeterminism need not always make any difference to how we deliberately act. Minute variations in the positions of various tiny particles may make no difference to whether or not, say, I deliberately raise my hand. Events at the macroscopic level might still be largely predetermined. Many or all of our actions could still be fixed in advance by causes outside our control. In which case, the causal predetermination of our actions could still remain a serious possibility – and so, if Incompatibilism is true, a real threat to our freedom.

But is the causal predetermination of our actions really so serious a possibility? No one has actually shown that determinism holds at the level of human action. Our actions are often predictable. Yet these predictions generally fall short of certainty. We find tendencies that many human actions follow. But these do seem to be tendencies only, not iron laws, and individual actions can still break the pattern. Belief in the wide-scale predetermination of human actions remains no more than a guess or speculation – a speculation that as yet remains not even probable, still less proved.

The threat of chance and unintelligibility

There is a deeper worry about freedom. Incompatibilism says that we cannot be free if determinism is true. But, as we are now about to see, it seems that we also cannot be free if determinism is false – and that this must be true on any view, whether we are incompatibilists or not. In which case if Incompatibilism is true we cannot be free at all. Freedom is impossible.

Suppose, as incompatibilist freedom would require, that our actions are not determined in advance. Then that seems to mean that how we finally act is a matter of simple chance. For there are but these two alternatives. Either an action is causally determined. Or, to the extent that it is causally undetermined, its occurrence depends on chance. But chance alone does not constitute freedom. On its own chance comes to nothing more than randomness. And one thing does seem to be clear. Randomness, the operation of mere chance, clearly excludes control. For example, if we are to count as exercising control over a process, that process cannot simply be developing at random. If a process is just random, then it must be taking place outside our control. Randomness is at least as much a threat to freedom – to our exercising control over how we act – as determinism might be. If our actions are no more than chance occurrences, then how can our action involve an exercise of control on our part?

The worry goes deeper. It is not simply that undetermined actions look no better than random. It seems that if what we think of as our actions were undetermined, they could not really be *actions* at all – they could be no more than mere blind motions.

Suppose, for example, that my hand goes up. What has to be true if my hand going up is to be, not a mere happening, but a genuine *action*, something that I intentionally do, a deliberate raising of my hand by me? Plausibly for me to count as raising my hand intentionally, there must be a purpose behind my hand going up. If I am intentionally raising my hand, I must be doing so for the sake of some goal or end. Perhaps I am raising my hand simply for its own sake – just for the sake of raising it. Or perhaps I have some further purpose in mind. Perhaps I am raising my hand in order to signal to you. But there had better be some purpose in what I am doing if it is to count as a genuine action – a deliberate and intentional doing of something by me.

What makes an action a genuine action, then, is that it is intelligible as something done by us deliberately, in order to attain some end or outcome. Action must always be something intelligibly purposive. It must always be directed at some goal or other – that is so whether the action's goal lies beyond it, or whether the action is merely being performed for its own sake. What, then, makes it true that our action is aimed at a given goal? What for example makes it true that when I raise my hand I am doing it in order to signal to you? Surely that I am performing the action out of a particular desire or motivation – a desire for or motivation towards that very goal. If my raising my hand is to count as having signalling to you as its goal, it must be my desire to signal to you that is causing my hand to go up. Movements of our body that are not caused by our desires – that occur whether or not we want them to – are not goal-directed actions, but mere blind motions such as twitches or reflexes.

To the degree that our actions are undetermined, so they will fail to be influenced by our prior desires, and the less how we move about and do things will depend on what beforehand we desire or want. And that means that these so-called actions will look less like genuine actions – and more like blind motions or reflexes. And how can blind motions or reflexes be free? How can blind motions or reflexes be genuine exercises of our control?

It seems then that if Incompatibilism is true, we cannot be free. For either our actions are causally predetermined, in which case – Incompatibilism says – they are imposed on us by past history, and we cannot be performing them freely. Or our actions are undetermined, in which case – on any view, it seems – they are no more than blind, random happenings and only actions so-called. In which case, again, we cannot be performing actions freely.

Compatibilism and Scepticism

Libertarianism is, for most of us, the natural theory of freedom. But that does not make Libertarianism true. For Libertarianism, we now see, faces more than one problem. It is not just that libertarians must believe that causal determinism is false – that our actions are not causally determined in advance. For all we know, that belief may well turn out to be true. There is another, more serious problem facing Libertarianism. Suppose causal determinism is indeed false. Libertarians must be able to explain how the causally undetermined events that they see as free actions really are that: genuine free actions. They must explain how, despite its being to some degree chancy whether they occur, these purported free actions differ from movements, such as reflexes and twitches, that are blindly random. But Libertarianism has not yet provided this vital story – a story of how incompatibilist freedom can be embodied in action that, though as causally undetermined as any mere chance motion, is nevertheless genuine free action. Libertarianism needs to explain how an action can be causally undetermined by past events without, however, being merely random or blind. And many philosophers have doubted that any such story can be given.

For this reason, despite our naturally libertarian intuitions, many, perhaps most, modern philosophers are inclined instead to *Compatibilism* or to *Scepticism*.

Compatibilism says that the up-to-us-ness of our actions – our freedom to act otherwise – is entirely compatible with our actions having been all along predetermined by causes outside our control. Freedom and causal determinism are perfectly consistent. Indeed, for the reasons already mentioned, compatibilist philosophers have even maintained that freedom positively requires that our actions be causally predetermined: to avoid being merely random and unintelligible, our actions must be guided and determined by our prior desires.

And for the last 200 years Compatibilism has had powerful support among English-speaking philosophers. There have even been times, as for much of the 20th century, when Compatibilism was the clearly dominant philosophical theory of human freedom. Much discussion of the free will problem in the 20th century was about trying to show that, after all, whatever our ordinary intuition might say to the contrary, freedom of action really is consistent with causal determinism.

But the fact remains that our natural intuitions are incompatibilist. If our actions are genuinely free, how can they be determined in advance? So other philosophers have continued to resist Compatibilism, insisting that freedom is inconsistent with

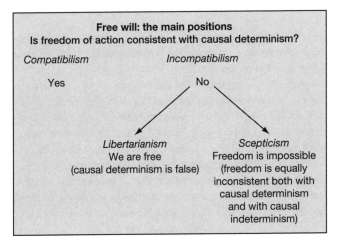

Free will: the main positions
Is freedom of action consistent with causal determinism?

Compatibilism   *Incompatibilism*

Yes   No

Libertarianism   *Scepticism*
We are free   Freedom is impossible
(causal determinism is false)   (freedom is equally
                                   inconsistent both with
                                   causal determinism
                                   and with causal
                                   indeterminism)

determinism. But these philosophers are not libertarians. For they say that freedom is inconsistent with indeterminism too. For the reasons given above, these philosophers think that undetermined actions would indeed be no more than blind, random motions. In other words, many modern philosophers combine Incompatibilism with Scepticism. Freedom, they maintain, is inconsistent both with determinism and with indeterminism; and so freedom is impossible.

The free will problem and its history

We naturally believe in our freedom – that it really is up to us which actions we perform. We also naturally impose an incompatibilist condition on that freedom. For us to be free, our actions cannot have been causally determined in advance by events long before our birth. Many of us, then, are natural libertarians. The trouble is that there appears no consistent model to be had of how freedom so conceived can be exercised through how we act. There seems to be no plausible libertarian account of what human action involves, and how it can be within the control of human agents. If no such account can be provided, we have a choice: seeking refuge in Compatibilism, or lapsing into Scepticism.

This is the free will problem as it now exists. It seems something of a philosophical trap – a trap with no obvious exit. The problem looks as though it has no freedom-friendly solution. But freedom was not always seen as posing this sort of insoluble problem. The free will problem as it now exists is a peculiarly modern problem, and it has a history. It has emerged as a result of a series of important changes in the way philosophers think, about freedom, about action, and about morality. It is these changes that have made it especially hard to make sense of human freedom – and that have left Libertarianism, in particular, looking like an indefensible doctrine. And these changes have mainly occurred in the last 400 years, since the Middle Ages. Medieval philosophy did not see human freedom as a problem quite as modern philosophers do.

It is true that medieval theories of human freedom were very different from any found in modern philosophy. But I shall still be examining these medieval theories in later chapters. And that is because the Middle Ages have much to teach us. Of course we cannot go back and think today exactly as the medieval philosophers once did. Many of the changes in thinking that have occurred since are irreversible. But not all intellectual changes are for the better, and some can and should be reversed. We especially need to understand the medieval tradition and how modern philosophy left it behind if we are to understand the modern free will problem – and escape the intellectual trap it imposes.

In the rest of this book I shall not only be explaining in detail how the modern free will problem has arisen, and why it has so far resisted solution, going into the libertarian, compatibilist, and sceptical positions in detail. I shall also try to persuade you that the idea of freedom is not nearly in so bad a condition as many suppose.

In particular, we have no compelling reason to abandon our libertarian intuitions. There really is a coherent account of how incompatibilist freedom can be exercised in human action. So there is certainly nothing internally confused or contradictory in our natural belief that we enjoy such a freedom. It is at least very possible that how we act is indeed up to us in just the way that we ordinarily suppose.

And that is all to the good. For I shall also be suggesting that freedom really is of moral significance after all. The idea that we are in control of some of what we do – that which actions we perform really is up to us – is at the heart of our moral thinking. If the idea of freedom is incoherent, an important part of our morality is incoherent.

Chapter 2
Freedom as free will

The unfreedom of animals

So far we have been looking at the relation between freedom and determinism. But there is another important aspect to freedom that has not yet been discussed – the relation between freedom and reason. To see how important reason might be, we need to consider some beings who certainly perform actions, but who do so without having the control over how they act that we humans possess over our actions. We need to consider the animals.

I am not claiming that all non-human animals lack freedom. For example, it is a matter of dispute exactly how intelligent chimpanzees and dolphins really are – and perhaps they will turn out to be free agents too. I suspect, in fact, that chimpanzees and dolphins are not intelligent enough in the particular ways needed for freedom, but this is not the place to argue the matter. We do not yet know enough about precisely how capable these higher animals really are. There are however other, much less sophisticated animals whose capacities fall very far short of our own, and who do clearly lack freedom of action as a result.

Consider sharks, for example. Sharks seem to perform actions – actions that are at least very analogous to ours. For example, a feature common both to shark and human actions is purposiveness:

the pursuit of an end or goal. We reach to the supermarket counter in order to get that loaf which we have just seen. The shark doubles back in order to get that fast-moving little fish which it has just spotted. Both shark and human are acting purposively, and both are trying to get something that they want.

With this purposiveness comes some sort of capacity for believing and desiring, even if, in sharks, these beliefs and desires may be fairly primitive. How better to explain why the shark doubles back to catch that fish than by supposing that there is some goal that it wants – to eat the fish – and something that it has just perceived or come to believe – that the fish is now over there? Guided by its beliefs about where the fish is, the shark's desire for food causes it to turn this way and that; and this effect of the desire on the shark's motion is what makes it true that the shark is acting purposively, that the shark's doubling back is directed at the goal of catching the fish.

A shark may hold beliefs and desires, and it may perform goal-directed actions as we do. Yet is a shark in control of its actions as we are? Is a shark really free to act otherwise than it actually does?

It is very natural for us to suppose not. But why? If we do naturally incline to deny that sharks are free agents, this cannot simply be because we believe that the shark's actions are causally predetermined. For we cannot be sure that the shark's built-in desires and instincts do determine its actions in advance. In any case, the causal predetermination of a shark's actions is not the issue. Even if we did learn that the shark's movements were sometimes undetermined, we would not conclude that therefore they must be free. We would simply conclude, in this case, that it was sometimes just a matter of chance, or quite random, what movements the shark would make. And to be moving around merely randomly, as we have already seen, is not the same as exercising control over how one acts.

Freedom and practical reason

A more plausible explanation why sharks are not free agents has to do with a shark's capacity for reason, or rather with its clear lack of it. To have genuine control over how we act requires that we have a capacity to act rationally – to act on the basis of informed reasoning about how we should act. But sharks lack any such capacity to reason about how to act. Sharks' actions are guided by instinct and not reason. Therefore it is not up to them which actions they perform.

A capacity to reason or deliberate about how to act involves far more than holding simple shark desires for food, and simple shark beliefs about where the food is. First, it involves a capacity to learn – to be flexible in the way that one responds to practical problems, both adapting to the unexpected, and also responding in new and better ways to old and already familiar problems. Sharks are not obviously inquisitive and inventive learners. Sharks do not obviously possess much of this intellectual flexibility.

Secondly, this intellectual flexibility must be linked to a capacity to understand and respond to practical problems as practical problems. When we face a question of what to do, we can understand it as such, as a practical problem, a problem about how to act. We are able to think of ourselves as having a choice between a variety of possible actions, and as therefore faced with the question of which action it would be best for us to perform – a question to which there can be an argued and right answer.

So we really can reason about how to act. We can actually ask ourselves which action is most worth performing, and then look for justifications or reasons why we should perform this action rather than that. These justifications are going to come from various possible goals or ends – goals that are worth attaining, and which performing the right action would allow us to attain. So, as reasoners, we are able to consider which goals are most worth attaining, and which actions would best enable us to attain them. It is in this way that we reflect upon our actions and evaluate them as more or less worth doing, as more or less justified.

It is this ability to recognize a justification for performing a particular action as a justification, and to appeal to such justifications in wondering about which actions are most worth performing, that gives us our capacity for rationality. And it is this capacity that a shark lacks. Sharks plainly do not think about justifications for and against the actions that they perform.

Why does it matter to freedom whether we can reason about how to act, whether we have this reflective understanding of practical problems as practical problems? The answer is simple. To be exercising control over something involves, at the very least, giving it deliberate guidance and direction. Our own actions, then, must in particular be things that as free agents we can deliberately guide and direct. But such deliberate guidance is impossible if we cannot even think of our own actions as needing guidance and direction, and have no idea of what such guidance and direction would involve. Free agents have to be able to think of there being more or less justified ways of acting, and to understand what is involved in arguing for the worth of doing this rather than that. Free agents need to be able to reason about their own practice – about how to act. They need, as philosophers put it, a capacity for practical reason.

Freedom and the will

Besides our capacity for performing actions, we also have a capacity for taking and arriving at decisions about how we shall act. As I put it in the last chapter, we also have a *will*. And this capacity for decision-making or will is clearly connected with our capacity for practical reason. The two capacities go together. To be able to deliberate about how it is best to act, and then to act on the basis of this deliberation, all this is precisely what it is to be a genuine decision-maker. This decision-making capacity – this capacity to make up our minds – follows from our ability to recognize and reflect on practical problems as practical problems. So if freedom depends on practical rationality, it also depends on what goes with practical rationality – on possessing a will. And sharks who are unfree because they lack our capacity for practical reason likewise lack our capacity for decision-making. Unlike us, sharks are unfree because they cannot go in for making up their minds about what to do.

The notion that humans possess a will arises, then, out of the very idea that we, as humans, have a capacity for rationality. To have a will, to be capable of decision-making, is to be capable of being moved into action by our reason, by our capacity to understand some goals as good or worth attaining, and by our capacity to see actions as providing better or worse ways of attaining these goals.

That at any rate is how the term 'will' was once used by philosophers. In medieval philosophy, for example, the Latin term *voluntas* or will served to pick out our decision-making capacity, the capacity that we have to be moved to action by our reason. That is why another Latin term that many medieval philosophers used for the will was *appetitus rationalis* – the rational appetite, or the reason-involving motivational capacity. To be a decision-maker is to possess an *appetitus rationalis*, a capacity to decide or move oneself to do this rather than that on the basis of reasoning about how to act.

In the last chapter we saw that philosophers have long referred to freedom of action as free will; as if our freedom of action were a freedom specifically of the will, a control over which decisions we took. And that is because in the Middle Ages, as rather less commonly since, many philosophers genuinely believed in an identity of our freedom of action with a freedom of decision-making. Were they right to do so?

Ordinary opinion certainly looks as though it is on the side of such an identity. For ordinary opinion suggests that as free agents we must also be free decision-makers. Consider – going just by your natural intuition – at what point in the process of deciding and acting your freedom begins. For example, suppose that in the morning, just as you get up, you take a decision about what you will do in the afternoon. You decide to go the bank in the afternoon, as opposed to just staying at home and reading. This decision taken in the morning then determines or leads you, in the afternoon, actually to go to the bank. What in this process do you control?

Plausibly not just whether, in the afternoon, you actually go to the bank. Equally up to you – equally within your control – is your decision, taken in the morning, to go to the bank. When you get up, it is entirely up to you – within your control – whether you decide to go to the bank or decide to stay at home. How you decide to act is intuitively as much up to you – as much within your control – as are the subsequent actions that result from what you decide.

Not only that, but it is hard to see how you could have the action control without the decision control. Imagine that the decisions which guide and determine your actions were just passive occurrences that come over you, like feelings, entirely outside your control. Imagining this, it is hard to hold on to the thought that, nevertheless, the actions which result are still within your control. If your decision to go to the bank is like a feeling, something which just happens to you, so that you have no control over whether you take it, and it is this uncontrolled feeling that determines whether you go to the bank, how can whether you go to the bank be within your control?

Finally, the following is just a natural thought to think, something that we ordinarily do believe. Surely we think this: that it is genuinely up to us how we act only because we can decide for ourselves how we shall act, and it is up to us which such decisions we take.

It seems then that, as we ordinarily conceive things, our freedom of action depends on a freedom of decision-making in particular. Now our capacity for decision-making, our will, is a mental or psychological capacity. And that means that our ordinary conception of freedom of action is what I shall term a *psychologizing* conception: it makes the freedom even of a bodily action such as whether or not we walk to the bank, depend on a prior strictly psychological freedom, on a freedom of whether or not we decide to go to the bank.

It also follows that there is an important complexity to our ordinary conception of action. Freedom or control, we have seen, is exercised in and through action. But if, prior to performing any of the actions between which we are to decide, we can already be exercising control over which decisions we take, then it must be true that decisions are themselves actions. If just as I control whether or not I go to the bank, I also control whether or not I decide to go to the bank, then taking a particular decision to act must itself be an action – my own deliberate doing. Besides the actions between which we decide, such as going to the bank or staying at home, there are other actions that we perform first: actions of the will, action-generating actions of decision, such as deciding to go to the bank or deciding to stay home.

In the rest of this book I shall be making use of an important term: *voluntary action*. By *voluntary actions* I shall mean simply the kinds of action between which we decide. Voluntary actions are those actions, such as going to the bank or staying at home, that we can and do perform on the basis of a prior desire or decision to perform them. They are called voluntary just because they are actions that are wanted or willed and decided on – because they can and do result from the prior operation of a *voluntas* or will to perform them.

It appears then that, besides our voluntary actions, the actions that we perform because we wanted to or decided to perform them, there is also a prior category of action. This category is made up of actions of the will itself, actions of deciding to perform this voluntary action or that – such as the action, say, of taking a decision to go to the bank.

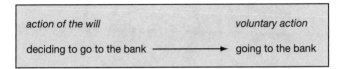

action of the will   voluntary action

deciding to go to the bank ——————▶ going to the bank

We need to understand the relation of these decisions, these actions of the will itself, to the voluntary actions that they produce and explain.

The free will tradition in the Middle Ages

In the Middle Ages, philosophers such as Aquinas and Scotus effectively identified freedom of action with freedom of will. Our freedom of action was based on a freedom of decision-making – on its being up to us how we decided or chose to act. And this basing of freedom of action on freedom of will was explained in terms of a highly distinctive and *will-based* theory of action. Human action and its freedom were taken by medieval philosophers to involve the exercise of our capacity for practical reason, and on our possession and exercise of the will in particular. The free exercise of the will – of our capacity to be motivated by reason – lay at the heart of every deliberate human action.

I have called the actions that we might want to perform and between which we eventually decide – the actions that we can perform on the basis of wanting or deciding to do so, such as raising one's hand, thinking about what to do next summer, going to the bank, and so forth – voluntary actions. Then, according to this will-based theory of action, when fully deliberate or intentional our voluntary actions always result from prior actions of the will, from

2. St Thomas Aquinas, woodcut of 1493

actions of decision or choice by which we decide to perform this voluntary action or that. According to the medieval theory, not only is every voluntary action preceded by an action of the will itself – an action of decision or choice which causes that voluntary action to occur. It is these initial actions of decision or choice which constitute our action in its primary and immediate form. Voluntary actions occur just through the effects of these initial actions of the will.

Let us take the example of a simple voluntary action: walking to the bank. When we perform an action such as this, according to the medieval will-based theory, we perform it in the following way. First, we *will*, we decide or choose, to walk to the bank – a decision or choice which counts by its very nature as a fully deliberate or intentional human action. Then this decision has the appropriate effects – the very effects that we have decided or chosen to occur. The decision causes our legs to move in the way that they must if we are to walk to the bank. And because these effects result from a decision that they should, we count as deliberately walking to the bank. To perform a deliberate action such as walking to the bank is to perform it on the basis of, through the effects of, a deliberate action of deciding so to act.

Intentional or deliberate action begins with deciding to act – the decision counting, immediately and inherently, as an action of ours. What we do voluntarily then counts as an action of ours only as an effect of this prior action of deciding. Action in general is performed entirely through the performance of actions specifically of the will.

It follows from this account of action that action can only be free to the degree that the will is free. Since all action is performed in and through performing actions of the will, our control of our action is exercised entirely as a control specifically of what we decide or will. Freedom of action is, in essence, freedom of will.

What of animal action? According to the medieval free will tradition, animal action was quite different from human action. Animal action was unfree, precisely because as non-rational beings animals were supposed to lack a will. And that meant that all animal actions were merely versions of shark actions. Animal movements were caused by nothing more than non-rational desires or passions, as guided by sensory beliefs or perceptions. No proper reasoning, and so certainly no decision-making, and therefore no freedom, was ever involved.

Jean DUNS dit SCOT
nomme le Docteur Subtil Religieux de
l'Ordre de St François né en Ecosse et
mort à Cologne en 1308, agé de 35 ans.

à Paris chés Daumont rue St Martin

Dans les tems ou la Scholastique
Ne cherchoit d'autre apuy que la Dialetique,
Par ses raisonnements pleins de Subtilité
Scot consacra son nom à l'immortalité.

Cacon

3. Duns Scotus

Decisions and intentions

To understand this free will tradition in more detail, let us look more closely at decisions. Decisions have two important properties. The first and most obvious is that they determine which voluntary actions we end up performing. The point of taking decisions about how we shall act is, after all, precisely to settle or determine what, at the level of voluntary action, we shall do.

Sometimes we take decisions at the very time of the voluntary action decided upon. You make me an offer, now, on a take it or leave it basis, and my decision to convey acceptance or refusal of the offer is carried out by me immediately. I accept or I refuse, depending how I decide, at once.

But other decisions are taken by us long before we get round to doing what we have decided. We take decisions in the winter about where to go on holiday in the following summer. And these decisions allow us to plan our action effectively. By deciding now that this summer I shall go on holiday in Spain rather than in Germany, I leave myself able to devote my resources and time to the preparations necessary for a Spanish holiday. I make bookings in Spanish hotels, buy Spanish guide and phrase books, and maps of Spain. I can do all this secure in the knowledge that I am not wasting my time and resources – that, thanks to my decision, I shall in fact be holidaying in Spain.

We take decisions in advance because we need to coordinate our voluntary actions through time. We need to make sure that how we act in the present fits with, or matches, how we act in the future. We need to make sure that, if we buy Spanish guide books now, rather than German ones, it is to Spain and not Germany that we shall be going in the future.

How does an advance decision determine how we shall act? The answer is, just as any decision does, by leaving us with an intention to act. Deciding to go to Spain in advance of actually going leaves one intending to go to Spain. To hold this intention involves remaining decided on or motivated to go to Spain – a state in which we continue until the time for the action decided upon arrives. A decision, then, is the formation of an intention, an intention that persists until, eventually, it causes the performance of the voluntary action decided upon.

Of course, a decision should not ensure that I act as decided whatever, no matter what happens in the future. I must be able to revise and abandon my decisions if I discover that the assumptions on which I based them were false or crucially incomplete. I should be able to change my mind about going to Spain if I suddenly learn that the whole Spanish hotel industry will be involved in a massive strike all summer. But failing the arrival of new information of this kind – information that would have led me to take a different decision had I possessed it from the outset – my decision should determine that I do act as decided. That, after all, is the point of taking a decision in advance: to fix or settle now what I shall be doing in the future.

The second feature of decisions is that they determine not only what voluntary outcomes we bring about – whether, for example, we actually go to Spain or not – but also our goals or purposes, what we are aiming at, in bringing those outcomes about. Indeed, it is our goals or purposes that decisions determine immediately; the determination of the eventual voluntary outcomes is secondary.

The immediate effect of my decision to go to Spain – an effect it has even before it gets me actually to go to Spain – is to leave me with one goal or aim in particular, a goal that I now have as my purpose. My goal now is that (exactly as I have decided) I do go to Spain. I have said that decisions induce intentions, that to decide to go to Spain is to form an intention to go to Spain. This term *intention* is another name for the state of having something as one's goal. In immediately leaving me intending to go to Spain, my decision leaves me with going to Spain as my goal. And only through being so directed at the goal or end of going to Spain – only through holding the intention to go – do I end up actually going to Spain. This goal or intention of going to Spain is then inherited and shared by whatever voluntary actions I perform in carrying out the decision. So when, in carrying out my decision to go to Spain, I buy an airticket for Spain, that action of buying the airticket will likewise be directed at the goal of my going to Spain.

We can now understand better the idea that freedom of action is initially and immediately exercised as freedom of will. The idea is that our freedom, and our capacity for agency, is initially exercised in decision-making, in the free action of adopting goals or aims. It is this initial action of adopting goals or aims which then determines our voluntary action into the future: what voluntary outcomes we eventually produce.

Morality as a morality of goals and purposes

If freedom of action consists in freedom of will that then means that our control over our voluntary actions also involves control over our aims – over the purposes for which we act. Not only do we have control over whether we actually help others or not. Prior to that we must also have control over whether we aim at helping them or not; indeed, whether our primary aim is the good of others, or only our own good. This doctrine that we control action-purposes or goals, and not just action-outcomes, is a very important idea. It was an idea that was very important to medieval moral theory – partly because the idea was and still is very important to moral common sense.

Medieval moral theory took very seriously the idea of our moral responsibility for our actions. Morality was seen as presenting us with obligations or duties – obligations or duties that addressed our capacity for free action, and that we could be blamed and held accountable for not keeping. It was generally agreed that we could be under such obligations at all only because we had a genuine control of how we acted; and we were under an obligation to exercise that freedom well, and not badly.

Medieval moral philosophy understood this morality of obligation entirely in terms of its will-based model of human action. Since the immediate exercise of our freedom was in decision-making – in aim or goal adoption – the first and fundamental moral obligation that we were under was an obligation to adopt the right aims or goals.

Medieval philosophy worked within the framework of Christianity. And so it was Christianity that dictated what these right aims or goals were understood to be. 'Love one another' was Christ's famous summation, in the New Testament, of our moral obligations in general towards others. Within the medieval tradition, this obligation to love was understood as involving an obligation to adopt the good of others as our aim or purpose: to decide to help others and to benefit them.

This is a rather different moral theory from those current in modern English-language philosophy. It depends on our believing that our freedom is exercised as a freedom of will. And this, we shall see, is a view of our freedom that is not generally accepted, either by modern compatibilists or by modern incompatibilists.

But we should remember that common-sense intuition is not so distant from the medieval theory. We do ordinarily think of decision-making, goal adoption, as itself a free action. And in ordinary life obligation does take in goals or purposes as well as actual outcomes. Indeed, in morality, it is arguably with people's goals or purposes that we are primarily concerned.

Suppose Fred selfishly and ungratefully fails to help his mother. We can simply blame him for not producing the right voluntary outcome, for not helping: 'You ought to have helped. It's wrong not to help her.' But we can equally well blame Fred for his selfish ingratitude, for failing to have any concern for his mother after she has done so much for him: 'You hard-hearted bastard' – we might say – 'you don't care. But you ought to be concerned for your mother. After all she's done for you, it's wrong just to be concerned for yourself. It's wrong of you to be so selfish.' In the second case we are delving deeper into what makes Fred so blameworthy: namely that, not only is he not helping, but that in so doing he is motivated by a selfish lack of gratitude, by a morally outrageous indifference to his mother. Fred's only purpose in life is his own good. He does not aim at furthering his mother's interests at all. That is what we are blaming Fred for: his selfishness, or the fact that his only final goal or purpose is his own self-interest.

Notice that we can go on blaming Fred for being so selfish even if, finally, he does do something that helps his mother. Suppose Fred does help in the end. This help might still be provided by Fred only in order to further his own interests – such as to ensure that he does not get cut out of his mother's will. If this is clearly Fred's real purpose in helping, we will go on blaming Fred 'for being such a bastard' even though he has finally helped his mother. And this is because what we are fundamentally blaming him for – his selfishness – has not gone away. We are fundamentally blaming Fred for being so selfish, a selfishness of which Fred's initial failure to help was only a symptom.

In ordinary life, we do blame people for aiming at the wrong goals, and not aiming at the right ones. We do blame people just for being selfish, and for their indifference to others. Making sense of this goal- or aim-related blame need not be a problem – if, as the medievals once did, we can understand the adoption of goals or purposes as an exercise of freedom. Fred can be directly responsible and to blame for his selfishness if this selfishness is his own free doing and lies directly within his control – if it consists in his freely intending only his own good, and not the good of others as well.

The free will tradition and medieval metaphysics

The medieval free will tradition identified freedom of action with freedom of will. And that, we have seen, is because it had a distinctive model of human action as consisting primarily in the exercise of a power of choice, of decision-making. This model dominated medieval action theory; and it looks in some respects close to common sense. At any rate, we too think of ourselves as free agents only because we can decide or choose how we shall act, and because it is up to us which actions we decide to perform.

But in many other respects medieval action theory was very different from much that we now believe. First, the business end of action was located entirely inside the will. All we ever do directly, on the medieval theory, is decide to perform this action rather than that. The rest of what we do counts as our deliberate and intentional doing only indirectly, as nothing more than an intended effect of our having first decided to do it.

But this is not quite what we ordinarily believe. Once I have taken a decision, say to cross the road, my direct involvement in action is not then over, the rest being up to nature. For when eventually I do act as decided and actually cross the road, my crossing of it is not something I am merely passively impelled into by my earlier decision to cross. As I actually cross the road, I am again directly involved in deliberately doing something, in a further exercise of my capacity for agency beyond and additional to that of my earlier decision so to act. And that is because my control over whether I cross the road is not exercised only indirectly and in advance – only through some previous decision to cross and its effects – but is also being exercised directly by me as I cross. This means that the voluntary action is more than just an effect of an earlier action that was performed entirely inside my head. It is also a further and direct involvement on my part in agency, something over which I am exercising direct control as I do it. Or so it seems to common sense. And so any credible account of the common-sense conceptions of freedom and agency should maintain. Perhaps it is true that to be possessed at all freedom must be exercisable in and through decisions of the will, through actions of decision-making and intention-formation. But freedom cannot be exercised in and through decisions and intention-formations alone. It is also and as directly exercised in voluntary actions, in the actions intended that our decisions and intentions explain. And so voluntary actions must count as genuine and distinct actions in their own right. They do not occur merely as intended effects of actions of the will performed earlier.

So while doing justice to the agency of decision-making and intention-formation – the agency of the will itself – we also need to do justice to that of our voluntary action. For we do not want to end up with a view of action that is, as I shall put it, *volitionist* – which says that our real involvement in agency, our action proper, is wholly mental and occurs only within the will, voluntary actions occurring merely as its subsequent effects. Yet in general medieval action theory was profoundly volitionist. For most of the medievals, our immediate involvement in deliberate and intentional action was wholly at the point of deciding to do this rather than that.

And this was connected with a second feature of medieval psychological theory. The will – our decision-making capacity – was held to be something immaterial and non-physical. That was because the will was a capacity to respond to reason; and reason and capacities directly responsive to it could not, the medievals generally supposed, be embodied in matter. This included our capacity for intentional or deliberate action, a capacity that the medievals saw as essentially and necessarily a capacity to respond to practical reason, to rational standards on action. That meant that our immediate involvement in intentional action had likewise to occur outside any bodily organ. It could only take the form of decisions or acts of will – actions that were purely mental or psychological. Everything else we did intentionally could only count as such derivatively, through being intended effects of such acts of the will. And these initial decisions or acts of will really had to be completely non-physical. They could not be events of the brain, for example. The voluntary actions to which they led might occur physically – as when our legs move as we walk to the bank. But the initial acts of will that gave rise to those voluntary actions had to be entirely spiritual and immaterial.

This belief in a total disembodiment or immateriality of our decision-making capacity is hard for us to share. We now have a knowledge of the brain not available in the Middle Ages. We can see, if only in outline, how the brain might be an organ of thought and reasoning, an organ that is material or physical. We see that the brain contains vastly complex neural networks conveying a plethora of electric charges or signals, changes in the distribution of which appear to be correlated with thought and mentality. We are inclined, therefore, to think that, like any other mental capacity, our decision-making capacity must somehow be embodied in the brain.

The medievals' belief in the immateriality of decision-making prevented them from seeing the free will problem as we do – as mainly a problem about how to reconcile freedom with the likelihood that actions are events within a physical world, subject like events of any other kind to physical causation. Instead, the medievals generally saw the world as a cosmic hierarchy – a hierarchy in which spirit or the immaterial outranked matter. And because spirit or the immaterial outranked matter, immaterial processes, processes such as reasoning or deliberate human action, could not be determined or necessitated by physical or material causes.

If anyone or anything could infallibly cause us to make a decision, that could only be God. And it was largely with reference to God that medievals saw our freedom as a problem. Three aspects of God in particular were seen to threaten the freedom of his human creation. These are God's omniscience, his knowledge of all truth, including truth about the future; God's impassibility, understood broadly as the idea that he cannot be passively affected by any external cause; and his omnipotent providence, the idea that everything that occurs happens by the will of God as all-powerful ruler of the universe.

Take omniscience first. God knows everything, including all our future actions. But how can this foresight be consistent with our freedom to act otherwise? If all along God has expected us to do A, and if God is incapable of error at any time, then how can we now be free to do B instead? It is not as if we are now in a position to change the past. It is not as if, when God has all along been expecting us to do A, we could ever change history to make it true instead that all along, from the very beginning of time, God has been expecting us to do B. Add to this the idea of God's impassibility and the problem deepens. For if God expects you to do A, and in fact you will do A, this cannot be a coincidence. There must be some connection between what God expects you to do and what you actually will do. Otherwise God's expectation would be not foreknowledge but a lucky guess. But what then is the connection? It cannot be this: the fact that you will do A has caused God to become aware of it, and that is how God knows. For then God would no longer be impassible. God would be causally affected by something outside him. It looks then as though the connection must be the other way round – through God affecting the world as its creator, and not the world affecting God. God's expectation that you will do A is no coincidence, no lucky guess, because it is based on God's decision that that is exactly how you will act – a decision which, thanks to God's omnipotence, you will infallibly carry out.

Which brings us to the problem caused for freedom by God's omnipotent providence. If all that happens occurs through God's decision that it should happen, a decision that God will infallibly carry out, and a decision on which all God's knowledge of the future is based, and if human actions are no exception to this, how can we be free to act otherwise? How can it be up to us how we will act if God has already infallibly foreordained and decided exactly how we will act?

The medieval free will problem was driven, then, more by theology than by physics. But it led to much less outright scepticism about freedom of the sort we find in modern philosophy. God and his nature were seen as posing intellectual difficulties for belief in human freedom. But these difficulties were generally seen as no more than that. And various ingenious theories were devised to surmount them.

In particular, some medieval thinkers did not see God's omnipotent providence as a threat to our freedom, but rather as its source. By deciding that you will perform an action God infallibly ensures that you will perform it. But this is no threat to your freedom. For God has made you by nature a free being. And God's influence over you as your creator will not threaten your nature but rather cause you to realize it. So by decreeing that you will do A rather than B, God ensures not only that A is what you will do, but that you will do A in a way consistent with your nature – which means that you will do A freely. The causal influence on you of a purely finite physical cause would be quite different in its implications for your freedom. That kind of material or physical causal influence, were it possible, would indeed threaten your freedom. But then physical causes were not generally seen as being able to determine immaterial actions of the will. And God's causal influence on such actions, as I have said, was sometimes seen as providing no such threat to freedom in any case – indeed, rather the reverse.

The medieval free will problem was, then, in many ways very unlike our own. It reflected very different beliefs about the human mind and about our place in the universe. To understand in detail exactly how the modern free will problem emerged, we shall need to turn to the 17th century. For in the 17th century the free will problem changed – and Compatibilism in its modern form first emerged. So first we need to look at Compatibilism generally – and then at Compatibilism in the very special form it takes nowadays, in the modern free will problem.

Chapter 3
Reason

Why Compatibilism?

Most people's immediate instinct is to suppose that freedom is inconsistent with causal determinism. If at the time of our birth our every future action was already causally predetermined, how could we ever be free to act otherwise? Compatibilism is not something naturally believed, but something that has to be taught – by professional philosophers, in philosophy books, and through philosophy courses.

So why do so many philosophers believe and teach the truth of Compatibilism? One obvious motive is this: to preserve human freedom from the threat that causal determinism could turn out to be true. But this is not the only motive, nor even the most important one. After all, causal determinism could well prove not to be true after all. Modern physics has certainly made it more likely that the world is not a deterministic system. But that has not lessened the popularity among philosophers of compatibilist theories of freedom. In any case, even if we do see causal determinism as a serious possibility, there is an alternative option. Instead of trying to explain how freedom really is compatible with causal determinism, we could try instead to explain why freedom might not matter after all. We could in particular seek to make sense of morality and human moral responsibility even in the absence of freedom. And, in fact, as we shall see, that is exactly what a number of philosophers have tried to do.

Worries about causal determinism alone are not what impel philosophers to Compatibilism. In fact the real appeal of Compatibilism lies deeper. And it has two quite separate, even conflicting, sources. Philosophers generally believe Compatibilism because they accept one of two quite dissimilar views of freedom.

One source of belief in Compatibilism is what I shall call a *rationalist conception of freedom*. In the last chapter we saw that there seems to be an important connection between freedom and reason. A free agent must have a capacity for reason and for acting on the basis of reason. A free agent is an agent capable of reasoning or deliberating about how to act, and of taking decisions about how to act on the basis of that deliberation. And this makes it natural to go further, and to see our freedom as nothing more than an expression of our reason. In effect, the temptation is simply to identify freedom with reason. On this view, to be a free agent is simply to be rational in one's action. And then, as I shall explain, this rationalist view of freedom, a view that identifies it with reason, will lead us into Compatibilism. This rationalist route into Compatibilism was especially important in the ancient world and in the Middle Ages, though it still matters today.

There is also a second and very different source of belief in Compatibilism – one that has become far more important since the 17th century, and which is central to the modern free will problem. Modern Compatibilism can also arise from *naturalism*. Naturalism is the conviction that humans are fully part of a wider material nature, and that humans are merely a more complex form of animal. So human action must be like and continuous with the actions of the lower animals. And human freedom of action must be a power over action not different in kind from other powers found in nature, including such power as the lower animals have over their actions.

It is clear that these two ways into Compatibilism are fundamentally different. Rationalist Compatibilism appeals to a tie between freedom and reason. And reason is something which, on the face of it, separates humans from the rest of nature, and certainly from markedly less intelligent animals such as sharks and mice. Whereas naturalist Compatibilism does not concentrate on reason or on anything that might separate humans from the other animals: rather the opposite. The naturalist tries to model human freedom as just another instance of powers and capacities that are not peculiar to humans but which, in some form or other, are to be found in wider nature. In its extreme form – a form to be found in the work of Thomas Hobbes, whose views I shall shortly be discussing – naturalist Compatibilism may even go as far as denying that freedom presupposes any capacity for rationality at all. Naturalism, that is, may even allow freedom to extend to non-rational animals. But even if naturalism does not go that far, it will still try to make out that human freedom does not involve any radical discontinuity between human nature and wider nature. It is the idea of a fundamental continuity between humans and the rest of nature that motivates naturalist Compatibilism. This chapter will look at the rationalist route into Compatibilism. Then Chapter 4 will examine the very different naturalist route.

Rationalist Compatibilism

Our freedom, we have already seen, plausibly depends on our having a capacity for practical reason. To have real control over one's actions requires that, at the very least, one be able to give one's actions deliberate guidance and direction. And that means being able to act on the basis of a conception of one's actions as needing such direction. If one is to be in control of how one acts, one must be able to see one's actions as standing in need of justification, and of being justified by some circumstances rather than others. Freedom requires that one be able to reason about how it is best for one to act, and to decide and act on the basis of such reasoning.

So freedom is tied to capacities for deliberation and decision-making – capacities whose very function is to ensure that we act rationally. For the point of bothering to deliberate and to take proper decisions about how to act is obvious enough. It is to ensure that we end up performing the right voluntary actions: voluntary actions that are rationally justified rather than otherwise.

So perhaps freedom, a power that comes to us with our capacity for practical rationality, just is that very same capacity for rationality. To be a free agent is just to be a rational agent. In which case, since they are the same, our freedom and our rationality should never conflict.

But this view that our freedom is just an expression of our reason – that freedom and reason are the same – is quite opposed to Incompatibilism. For Incompatibilism implies that freedom and reason certainly can conflict, as we shall see. If Incompatibilism is true, freedom cannot be the same as reason.

Take a case where, under the circumstances, there is a single most sensible thing to do – perhaps it might be taking the one medicine which, though nasty, will cure a particularly serious illness that I have. All the other options, taking other treatments or no treatment at all, are clearly less sensible. If so, the more reasonable I am, the less chance there should be of my failing to take my medicine. Irrationality or unreasonableness in an agent, after all, is nothing other than a propensity to fail to do the sensible thing, and to do the foolish thing instead. The more unreasonable I am, the greater this propensity; correspondingly, the more reasonable I am, so the propensity should be less and, ultimately, when I am fully reasonable, it should be completely absent. If I am completely reasonable, there should be no chance at all of my failing to do the sensible thing.

So if I am completely reasonable then, first of all, I must fully realize that taking my medicine is the right thing to do; and then my realization that taking my medicine is the right thing to do must ensure that I take it. There should be no chance at all of my acting foolishly in this case. My very rationality must determine that I do the one sensible thing.

Causal determination of my decision by recognition of what I should do (no chance that I will fail to do what I recognise to be right)

Recognition that taking the medicine is the right thing to do ⟶ Deciding to take the medicine and taking it

But if the very fact of my rationality does ensure that I take my medicine, how, in incompatibilist terms, can I ever be free to act otherwise? Suppose I am completely reasonable. Then, if my disease needs to be cured, and can only be cured by taking this medicine, I must immediately realize this. My awareness that I should take the medicine must be something that I cannot help but possess. My situation must causally determine my beliefs about what I should do. And then my beliefs about what I should do must causally determine what I decide to do, and ensure that I stick with that decision and carry it out. Once I am aware of what I must do, there must be no chance whatsoever of my doing anything else. But then how, when I decide and act, can I still be free to decide and act otherwise? Incompatibilist freedom depends on my decisions and actions not being causally determined in advance. But being fully reasonable seems precisely to involve one's decisions and actions being determined in advance.

In which case if Incompatibilism is true, then the more reasonable I am, the less freedom I can possess – the less I can be in control of my actions. If I am totally reasonable, I must almost entirely lack control of what I do. For whenever I recognize that a given action is the right thing to do, I should have no freedom in the matter – my belief that that action is right should ensure I perform it, imposing that action on me. The only time when I would ever have any control over my actions would be in cases where, in a sense, the control matters less anyway. That would be in cases where I recognize that a number of options are equally sensible, so that it does not matter from the point of view of reason which option in particular I follow.

Possession of substantial incompatibilist freedom looks, then, as though it depends on my being to some degree unreasonable. Even when I recognize that a particular action is the right thing to do, if I am to possess incompatibilist freedom there must still be some chance that I may do the less sensible thing nevertheless. But then incompatibilist freedom is very far from being an expression of reason. Incompatibilist freedom is often at war with reason.

Many philosophers have thought that freedom cannot be in conflict with reason. And this conviction that freedom and reason cannot conflict has led them to reject Incompatibilism, and to adopt a rationalist form of Compatibilism. It is easy to see why. A tendency to irrationality is surely a weakness. But is not Incompatibilism tying the possession of freedom to just this weakness? And does not this turn freedom into a kind of weakness too? The rationalist compatibilist maintains that, properly understood, freedom – having real control over which actions we perform – is not a weakness but a strength. Freedom is a genuine *power* – a power that comes to us with rationality. It cannot therefore be a weakness based on irrationality. The capacity to act reasonably is what helps to give us freedom. But if so, complete reasonableness, this capacity in its most effective and complete form, cannot be what would take this freedom away.

There are modern philosophers who are still interested in exploring some form of rationalism about freedom. Thus in her *Freedom within Reason*, the American philosopher Susan Wolf explores what she calls the Reason view – the view that free will and responsibility consist in 'the ability to act in accordance with Reason' (p. 68), so that to be a free and responsible being is to have 'the ability to act in accordance with the True and the Good' (p. 73). Rationalism about freedom has also proved profoundly attractive to many Christian thinkers, for reason and freedom have historically been seen as forms of perfection. So God, in particular, as a wholly perfect being, must be both completely reasonable and completely free. It is certain and necessary from the outset that God will always do what is sensible and right; and yet God must also remain entirely free and in control of all that he does. We, of course, are not like God. In our case there is always a chance that we will act wrongly and foolishly. But this chance that we will act foolishly is a reflection of our imperfection and weakness. To be made perfect – to become good and reasonable as God is, and so to be similarly bound to act well – this will be our destiny in heaven. And, for many Christian thinkers, this destiny will be a liberation from weakness and so not the end of our freedom, but freedom in its most perfect form. If so, the freedom that we will enjoy must be consistent with the causal predetermination of our action, not incompatible with it. For it looks as though in heaven how we act will be determined in advance – by our very rationality.

Are freedom and reason ever the same?

Should we identify freedom with reason? If we do, we certainly will end up as compatibilists. For any substantial degree of incompatibilist freedom depends, as we have seen, on our beliefs about how we should act leaving it still chancy how we shall act – on there still being some chance that we will irrationally do what we should not do. And that chanciness, that propensity to behave foolishly, is in clear conflict with reason.

But it must be a mistake to identify freedom with reason. Freedom and reason cannot be the same. For one thing, decision and action is not the only area of our life where we exercise a capacity for rationality. We also do so in forming beliefs and desires, which can be reasonable or unreasonable just as our decisions and actions can be. But in the case of, say, belief, we do not generally regard the exercise of our rationality as an exercise of freedom. For we do not generally control which beliefs we form as we control which actions we perform.

When I believe, as I do, that I am sitting in my study and am surrounded by tables, books, and chairs; that outside my study, and extending far beyond what I can presently hear or see, is a whole city with millions of people in it – all this is a perfectly good exercise of my capacity for rationality. These beliefs that I form are a fully reasonable response on my part both to the evidence of my present experience and to what I remember of the past. But I certainly do not have any control over whether I form these beliefs. It is not up to me whether I believe that there are chairs in my room and that there are millions of people outside. My own capacity for reason imposes these beliefs upon me. It imposes these beliefs on me as obviously true, so that it simply is not within my control to think otherwise. In the case of beliefs, far from freedom being the same as reason, freedom – the freedom to believe otherwise than as I actually do – is something that reason prevents.

This suggests that we cannot identify freedom with reason – and not even with the special case of reason as it relates to action. For if reason is something that prevents freedom where belief is concerned, why should it be identical with freedom where action is concerned?

It is sometimes claimed that there is a fundamental difference between theoretical reason or reason as exercised in belief, and practical reason or reason as exercised in action. Theoretical reason always leaves it determinate what we should believe about a given matter. Reason never leaves it rationally open whether and what beliefs we should form. Take any factual claim, such that there are four chairs in the room. Then either the evidence will show that the claim is true – in which case reason requires us to believe it – or the evidence will show that the claim is false – in which case we should disbelieve it. And finally, if the evidence is unclear, reason again leaves it completely determinate what we should think. Reason requires us to remain doubtful.

Whereas in the practical case, the evidence can show that a number of alternative actions are equally good – or at least leave it unclear which action is better than which. If so, then reason leaves it open which action we should pick. Though on any one matter and at any given time only one of the theoretical alternatives of belief, disbelief, or doubt can ever be reasonable, a number of alternative actions can often be equally reasonable.

But this is not enough to explain how reason might amount to freedom in the practical case. It is clear enough why. Our belief in our freedom of action is not limited to cases where practical reason leaves the options indifferent. Freedom extends even to cases where practical reason is as limiting and determinate as theoretical reason can be. Even in cases where all the evidence points unambiguously to one particular action being the best action to perform, and we can see this perfectly clearly, we can still think of ourselves as free to act otherwise. Reason can leave it just as obvious to us that we should take some medicine, as that we should believe in the existence of a whole city beyond our room. But while reason imposes the sensible belief on us, it does not similarly impose the sensible action. Reason still leaves us free to act otherwise and against our own reason – as, unfortunately, we sometimes do. Though we are convinced that taking that nasty medicine is the best and right thing to do, we may still exercise our freedom not to take it. Because we expect it to be so nasty, we may freely choose to avoid the nasty option – even though we are firmly convinced that the nasty option is the best. We control how we act as we do not control what we believe – and that includes cases where reason clearly dictates which action we should perform.

Freedom and irrationality

The rationalist wants to identify freedom with reason, or at any rate with practical reason or reason as it relates to action. But it may be that the relation between freedom and reason is really much looser. It may be that freedom and reason are never the same; that freedom is an extra capacity that we possess over and above our capacity for rationality, a capacity for control that we possess only in relation to our action. In which case, though freedom of action may require a degree of rationality – though it may require a capacity deliberately to direct our voluntary actions through deliberation and decision – there may be no further connection between freedom and rationality than that. In which case freedom and reason may turn out to be in tension after all. It may be perfectly possible for freedom and reason to conflict.

Here is another way of looking at the matter. I have said that freedom depends on our having capacity for rationality. If that is so then freedom may equally depend on our having a capacity for irrationality too. This may seem excessively paradoxical. But it is in fact not too difficult to explain why freedom might equally depend on a capacity for irrationality. The key point is this. Genuine irrationality, real folly, or silliness, is possible only for beings that also have a genuine capacity for rationality. Take an animal that is clearly devoid of reason, such as a shark. As we have seen, a shark cannot reason about how it should act, or have any understanding that some ways of acting might be more sensible than others. And this certainly means that a shark cannot ever be said to be making wise choices, or to be acting sensibly. On the other hand it equally means that a shark cannot be said to be making silly choices or to be acting foolishly either. To be foolish or silly is not to be lacking in reason altogether; it is to be neglecting to use, or failing to use properly, a capacity for reason that one nevertheless does actually possess. Sharks are not irrational or silly beings. They are non-rational beings –

animals below any form of rationality or irrationality, just as much incapable of misusing reason as they are of using it.

The capacities for deliberation and decision-making that allow us to be rational are also the very capacities that allow us to be irrational. And perhaps these capacities help give us our freedom only because they as much permit irrationality as they permit rationality. And surely freedom often is possible only because irrationality is possible too – in precisely those cases where we face a choice, and where only one of the options is sensible or rational. For freedom, by its very nature, is a freedom to act otherwise. Freedom always involves more than one option by way of action being available to us. And that means that in all those cases where only one option is sensible, we cannot be free unless we are free to be silly as well as sensible.

To identify freedom with reason is in fact to deny the very nature of freedom. For in many situations following reason, being sensible, leaves us with only one option. Any alternative is excluded. But freedom by its very nature involves the availability of alternatives. To be free is for it to be up to us which actions we perform – and so it just is for more than one action to be available to us, whether that alternative is silly or sensible. This is why rationalist Compatibilism has often tried to detach what it calls 'freedom' from any idea of a freedom to act otherwise. God's freedom, freedom in its most perfect form, was supposed by the rationalist to exist without God being free to act in anything other than the most perfect way – in the way in which he actually acts. But to detach freedom from a freedom to do otherwise is really to change the subject. It is to abandon the idea of freedom, and replace it with the very different idea of reason and reasonableness. And the two ideas are not at all the same. To be reasonable is not necessarily to have any capacity to act otherwise. Indeed someone's rationality could in some cases perfectly well exclude the capacity to act otherwise. Take a case where acting otherwise would conflict with reason. In such a case someone might be so profoundly sensible as to be quite incapable of doing the silly thing. But to be free is always to have a capacity – a freedom – to act otherwise. That is just what freedom is – its being up to us which actions we perform, so that it is up to us whether we act in one way or in another.

Chapter 4
Nature

Thomas Hobbes

The 17th-century philosopher Thomas Hobbes began an intellectual revolution in the theory of human action. This new theory transformed not only the view taken of action, but also the whole free will problem. Hobbes's work changed our thinking about freedom, and even about morality.

This revolution centred on the relation between action and the will: Hobbes changed the way in which this relation was understood. As I explained earlier, the traditional view saw the human will – the human decision-making capacity – as a very special capacity indeed. It was a rational or reason-involving capacity that the other, lower animals entirely lacked. And the traditional view located human action within this capacity of will. Human action was supposed to occur in and through the exercise of our decision-making capacity.

Hobbes devised a completely new theory of human action. This theory downgraded the will. The will was no longer a special capacity that distinguished rational humans from non-rational animals, but became instead a capacity of a far more humble kind. The will was now to be no more than a basic appetitive capacity – a capacity for appetites or wants that humans and animals could perfectly well share. Hobbes then located all action, human and animal alike, entirely outside the will so understood. Action no longer occurred as an exercise of the will itself, but occurred instead only as a subsequent effect of the will's exercise. And almost all philosophers since have been influenced by his theory.

For Hobbes, man is just part of material nature. The world is no more than a collection of material bodies in motion, where every motion that occurs is causally determined to occur by some previous motion. The Hobbesian universe, then, is a material deterministic system. Humans are simply more material bodies within this system, albeit bodies of a highly complicated kind. Still, Hobbes maintains, human freedom does exist. Far from freedom being excluded by materialism and determinism, what freedom comes to can be entirely explained in materialist and determinist terms.

Central to Hobbes's theory is that humans only differ from other animals by being more complex versions of the same thing. The differences of intelligence and capacity between us and the animals are differences in degree, not differences of kind. Hobbes denies that we possess psychological faculties radically different from any found in the animals.

This new idea of human nature was quite different from medieval philosophy with its will-based action theory. For, of course, special faculties peculiar to humans were precisely what the traditional will-based action theory had always gone in for. On the will-based theory, human action is supposed to occur as a quite different kind of phenomenon from animal action. And that is because human action is supposed to involve a special capacity for free decision-making – a capacity that only humans possess.

4. Thomas Hobbes, *c.*1669–70, by J. M. Wright

Consider again how the traditional view runs. According to this, remember, humans are uniquely capable among the animals of exercising reason. So we alone can deliberate and decide what to do. And it is our decisions to do this rather than that – to raise our hand rather than lower it, say – which are our action in its primary form. That is, the rest of what we do is done only indirectly, through these actions of decision-making. The rest of what we do, the *voluntary* actions decided upon which execute our decisions – the actions of raising our hand or lowering it, and the like – occur as nothing more than effects of prior actions of decision or will. If I count as freely raising my hand, that is only because a freely taken decision on my part to raise my hand has caused my hand to rise. Since all action occurs as an exercise of the will, our freedom of action must similarly take the form of a freedom of will. Our freedom is always exercised through free decision-making.

<u>Human action – understood in will-based terms</u>

action of the will
(primary form of action)

voluntary action
(secondary form of action)

Deciding to raise one's hand ⟶ Raising one's hand

Animals are very different from humans on the traditional view. Animals lack any capacity for reason or rationality. Far from taking free, self-determined decisions, animals are driven by passive desires or appetites. Animal action is therefore restricted to what for humans was only a secondary form of action. Animal action is restricted to the category of what I have called *voluntary* actions. Animal actions are restricted to actions such as raising a hand, or a paw, which humans might perform on the basis of freely deciding to perform them, but which animals perform only on the basis of being driven by a brute desire to perform them. Animal action comes to nothing more than animals moving as their desires or wants drive them to move. It comes to no more than animal appetites or desires causing movements in animal limbs – which is why, according to

<u>Animal action</u>

passive desire

voluntary action

Wanting to raise one's paw ⟶ Raising one's paw

the traditional view, reasonless animals lack freedom of action altogether. Far from controlling which actions they perform, animals are driven by instinct.

What Hobbes essentially did was to retain the traditional theory of animal action, but extend it to include human actions as well. For Hobbes, human action is merely a more complex form of animal action. All action, both human and animal, occurs in precisely the same form – as voluntary action, and as a mere effect of passive desires or motivations. The only difference in the human case is that, thanks to our greater intelligence, the desires that cause our actions are more varied and sophisticated in content.

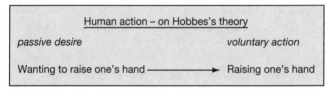

Human action – on Hobbes's theory

passive desire   *voluntary action*

Wanting to raise one's hand ⟶ Raising one's hand

Hobbes's first concern – and his most fundamental one – was to diminish the gap between the actions of humans and the actions of the lower animals. Hobbes wanted to establish that human action was wholly continuous with animal action. There was to be no difference in kind between action as performed by a human and action as performed even by a shark. Shark action, it seems, comes to no more than a very simple form of voluntariness. Shark action involves the shark being caused to do things by its desires to do them. The shark's pursuit of its prey involves nothing more than the shark being caused to pursue and eat by its desire to pursue and eat. If human action is to be the same kind of phenomenon, then it must similarly occur as nothing more than an effect of wants or desires.

Hobbes still claimed to allow for some sort of notion of the will – of decision-making and intention-formation. But in fact it is not clear that there was very much left of the notion. It is not obvious that Hobbes really believed at all in decisions as we ordinarily understand them. For Hobbes, decisions and intentions are no more than forms of desire. To decide or form an intention to do something is no more than to be overcome by a very strong desire to do it – a desire that is strong enough to override any opposing motivation we might have to act otherwise, and determine us to act exactly as desired. To take a decision to raise your hand is just to be overcome by a very strong desire to raise your hand – a desire strong enough to ensure that you actually raise it. This means that the will is nothing special. The will is just a capacity for ordinary desire or appetite. So since sharks have appetites and wants, they also possess wills as much as we do. And there is nothing free or self-determined about decisions, on Hobbes's view, any more than there is anything free or self-determined about humble wants or desires. Taking a decision is no more a deliberate action – no more something that we can do freely, which we have direct control over – than is feeling an urge.

Action, then, is restricted by Hobbes to action that is *voluntary* – to actions, such as raising a hand or crossing the road, which we perform on the basis of having decided or wanted to do them. In fact Hobbes explicitly *defines* action as 'what is done voluntarily'. For Hobbes, to perform an intentional or deliberate action is nothing more than to do something, such as raising your hand, on the basis of having decided to do it – or (what for Hobbes comes to the same thing) to be caused to do something by a prior desire or want to do it.

This identification of action with what we do voluntarily or on the basis of a prior desire or decision to do it has a fundamental consequence. It allows Hobbes to explain why, as he supposed, decisions can never be deliberate or intentional actions themselves.

As Hobbes observed, decisions are not themselves things we take voluntarily. My decision to raise my hand, for example, is not something I take on the basis of a prior decision to decide to raise my hand. As Hobbes put it, using the 17th-century term *willing* for our modern *deciding*:

> I acknowledge this liberty, that I can do if I will, but to say, I can will if I will, I take to be an absurd speech.

And Hobbes was surely right on one point at least. Decisions to act are not voluntary. They are not directly subject to the will. They cannot be taken just on the basis of prior decisions or desires so to decide. For example, I cannot decide that in precisely five minutes' time I shall then take a decision to raise my hand – and sensibly expect that in five minutes, at the appointed time, I shall take the decision decided upon, and take it voluntarily, just on the basis of my earlier decision that I shall take it.

And this is connected with another feature of decisions that also distinguishes them from what we really can do voluntarily – from what we really can do on the basis of a prior decision or desire to do it. Just as decisions are not directly subject to the will, so they are not directly subject to command. I cannot sensibly command you to take a particular decision, such as a decision to raise your hand, and then expect you to take the decision commanded exactly as commanded and simply in order to obey my command. Suppose, for example, I commanded you thus: 'In five minutes' time take a decision to raise your hand tomorrow – and then, after a further minute, abandon that decision, and instead decide not to raise your hand tomorrow. Then, after yet a further minute, abandon that decision too.'

You would surely react to my command with some bewilderment. You would be quite incapable of carrying it out. Decisions are not things that can be taken simply in order to obey commands that they be taken. The fact that decisions cannot sensibly be commanded is obviously connected with the fact that decisions cannot be taken voluntarily. For if decisions could be taken voluntarily, on the basis of a prior decision to take them, then you could perfectly well take decisions simply in order to obey my decision commands. You need only decide to take whatever decisions I commanded you to take, and then obeying my decision commands would be easy. Once I commanded you to take a particular decision, such as a decision to raise your hand, you would simply take that decision voluntarily, on the basis of a decision to take it, and as a means to fulfilling my command.

It is very clear why decisions cannot sensibly be commanded. If I want to get you to decide to raise your hand, I cannot just command you 'Decide to raise your hand!' To get you to decide to raise your hand, I have somehow to convince you that acting as decided, raising your hand, would be a good idea. I have to give you some reason to raise your hand. I have somehow to show or make it clear to you that raising your hand would have benefits.

One way to do that, of course, is to *make* it true, and obviously true, that raising your hand would have benefits. For example, I could offer you a reward for raising your hand. That could get you to decide to raise your hand. Or if I have the necessary authority to do so, I could simply issue a command. Not a command to decide to raise your hand, but a command that would give you a reason to act as decided and actually raise your hand. I could simply command you to raise your hand. Given this command, there would be one possible benefit to your raising your hand, one reason why you should raise it – namely, that in doing so you will obey my authority. And by giving you this reason to raise your hand, I could again get you to decide to raise it.

What moves one to take a particular decision then, to decide on a particular action, is not any command to take that decision, or any prior decision on one's own part to take it, but some reason for acting as decided – something good or desirable about the action decided on. What moves one to decide to raise one's hand is not any command so to decide, or any decision on one's own part so to decide, but something quite different – something good or desirable, not about taking the decision itself, but about performing the action to be decided upon, about actually raising one's hand.

So Hobbes was quite right about the non-voluntariness of decisions. We cannot take a particular decision to act at will, just because we have decided to take it. We should not be distracted from appreciating this by the fact that there is something else connected with decision-making that we can do voluntarily. This is not taking a particular decision to act, but something that is very easily confused with it but which is, nevertheless, importantly different – namely making up our mind one way or the other what to do.

I can perfectly well decide that in five minutes' time I will make up my mind one way or the other about whether to raise my hand – and then, in five minutes' time, make my mind up on the basis of that earlier decision. Making one's mind up one way or the other, then, is something that can be done voluntarily, on the basis of a prior decision to make one's mind up. But that does not show that the taking of a particular decision can be voluntary too. Making up my mind, after all, is a process. And it initially involves deliberating or at least seriously considering the options – something that is done preparatory to making any particular decision. It is this that can be done voluntarily. But which particular decision I then arrive at is not a voluntary matter. If when I make my mind up I decide to raise my hand rather than lower it, this is not something I can have done on the basis of some earlier decision to arrive at that particular decision rather than its opposite. I can decide in advance *that* I shall make my mind up; but I cannot effectively decide in advance *how* I will make my mind up. Deciding to do this rather than that is something entirely non-voluntary, just as Hobbes supposed. Deciding to do this rather than that is something I do in response to the options as I see them at the time – in response to their potential benefits, real or apparent – and not on the basis of some earlier decision to decide this particular way rather than the other.

Combined with Hobbes's new definition of intentional action as what we do voluntarily, on the basis of a decision or desire to do it, the non-voluntariness of decision-making has an obvious consequence. That I decide to do this rather than that, to raise my hand rather than lower it, can no longer be my own deliberate or intentional doing. Since it is non-voluntary, that I decide to do this rather than that is going to be something that happens to me, rather than anything that I intentionally do. Because they are non-voluntary, decisions cannot themselves be deliberate actions. So what the will-based theory takes to be the primary form of intentional action – the taking of a decision to do this rather than that – Hobbes denies to be an action at all. And if not an action, if not something done deliberately or intentionally, deciding to do this rather than that cannot be something we do freely either. There can no longer be any freedom of will. It can no longer be up to us which actions we decide to perform.

In fact Hobbes thought that the traditional will-based theory of action was thoroughly incoherent. The traditional theory explains what makes hand raising an intentional action by appealing to the fact that the hand's rising is a voluntary effect of a decision to raise it. But, unfortunately, the traditional theory seems then to have nothing very convincing to say about what makes the taking of that prior decision one's intentional action too. The only story available, so far as Hobbes could see, was the same kind of story already told about the hand raising. This is the story that appeals to voluntariness, to something's being an effect of a decision to do it. But in Hobbes's view, this is not a story we can tell to explain how decisions themselves are actions. And that is precisely because decisions are not voluntary. You cannot take a decision to raise your hand on the basis of having decided so to decide.

We can now see how very different Hobbes's theory of human

action is from the will-based theories that it was designed to replace. In Hobbes's theory, acting as decided – the voluntary production of outcomes – is not a secondary form of action, an action that we perform through a primary action of deciding to do it, but the only form of action that there is. When I voluntarily raise my hand, the only action which I perform is that voluntary action: the raising of my hand. My prior decision to raise my hand is not an action at all. That decision is nothing more than a strong desire that comes over me outside my control, and which then pushes me into action by causing my hand to rise up.

So the will-based theory of human action, a theory that takes action to be primarily an exercise of freedom of will, is being replaced by a quite different, Hobbesian picture. Human action is just us being pushed into motion by our wants. And this changes profoundly the view taken of human freedom.

For Hobbes, human freedom is no longer exercised as a freedom of will or of goal adoption. Nor does it depend on reason. Hobbesian freedom comes to no more than this: to there being no obstacles to the satisfaction of whatever desires we might happen to hold. It does not detract from our freedom that our actions might be causally determined in advance by our desires, by desires that have come over us and which are none of our doing. All that matters to freedom is that once a desire is held there should be nothing that could get in the way of its satisfaction. Freedom is nothing more than an unobstructed will – unobstructed will being of course understood by Hobbes as nothing more than unobstructed desire:

> *A* FREE-MAN, *is he, that . . . is not hindred to doe what he has a will to* . . . from the use of the word *Free-will*, no Liberty can be inferred of the will, desire or inclination, but the Liberty of the man; which consisteth in this, that he finds no stop, in doing what he has the will, desire, or inclination to doe.

And freedom, so understood, is clearly compatible with causal determinism. Hobbes's theory of freedom is evidently compatibilist. Suppose our every action turns out to have been causally determined in advance by desires that fate has imposed on us. For Hobbes, we can still be free. We can still be free provided there is nothing that would stop us from doing exactly as we want, once fate has led us to want to do it. It is not causal determinism that removes Hobbesian freedom, but restraints such as locked cell doors and ropes and chains – restraints that prevent us from doing what we want.

Moreover freedom is no longer limited to humans. Freedom on Hobbesian terms is also something that we can perfectly well share with the lower animals such as sharks. A shark too may have an unobstructed capacity to do or get what it wants. And an unobstructed capacity to do what one wants is all that freedom ever comes to. Not only is Hobbes a compatibilist, but his Compatibilism makes freedom an entirely natural phenomenon, common to humans and the lower animals alike.

Hobbes's theory of freedom is very striking. It seems to leave human freedom amounting to very much less than was previously thought. Indeed, some would say that human freedom seems to have disappeared. Instead we have the freedom of a marionette, its limbs jerked into motion by desires that, in effect, amount to forces applied to it, forces that lie outside its control. Much of the subsequent history of the free will problem in English-language philosophy has been a series of reactions to this brutally minimalist picture of freedom.

In fact, Hobbes can be seen as the inventor of the modern free will problem. In the Middle Ages, before Hobbes, the free will problem was centrally a problem about how human freedom was related both to human rationality and to the knowledge and action of an omnipotent and omniscient God. The central questions were these. How does the capacity for reason make humans free? And how is human freedom consistent with God's providential control of the universe and his foreknowledge of how we will act? After Hobbes, the free will problem increasingly becomes a quite new kind of problem – a problem about how to fit human freedom into a naturalist world picture. The question under debate increasingly becomes this. If humans exist as parts of a wholly material world of cause and effect, how is human freedom possible?

Hobbes and common sense

Many philosophers have been convinced by Hobbes. These philosophers agree that Hobbesian freedom, an unobstructed capacity for voluntariness, a capacity to act as we happen to want, is the only freedom there could ever be. Ideas of freedom as anything more are purely inventions. That freedom might depend on a special capacity for reason, or that it might depend on our actions not being determined in advance – all this is a fantasy.

And Hobbes's picture of what freedom might come to looks plausible enough once you accept his theory of action. Hobbes identifies action with voluntariness, with doing what we want because we want to do it. That essentially is all that Hobbes believes to go on when we act: our being driven into motion by our own desires. So what more could freedom, the self-determination that we exercise in our action, be but voluntariness?

According to Hobbes, to act is simply to do something on the basis of wanting to do it, and that is how we experience our own agency. The child wants to pick up that ball lying on the floor, and finds itself managing to pick the ball up just as it wanted to do. In managing to do what it wants, the child has had, if you like, its first experience of successful self-determination. And it is only from later reflecting on this experience of being able to act as we want that we ever gain any real understanding and knowledge of what self-determination is. Or so the Hobbesian would maintain. And this has an obvious consequence. If Hobbes is right about action, the only self-determination that we ever experience in our actions is a kind of voluntariness – doing what we want because we want to do it. And this means that ideas of freedom as anything more are quite unsupported by what we actually experience.

But ordinary opinion, let us be clear, is very obviously on the side of the supposed fantasy, and firmly opposed to Hobbes. As ordinarily understood, freedom certainly does involve more than a capacity to act as we want.

Hobbesian freedom, remember, is no more than unobstructed desire. The only thing, according to Hobbes, that can remove our freedom, is some obstacle to satisfying our desires. Our freedom can never be taken away by our desires themselves. But common sense thinks of freedom quite differently. It sees freedom as something that can perfectly well be taken away from us, not merely by obstacles to our desires, but by our desires themselves. Consider drug addicts, for example. A drug addict is a person imprisoned, not by obstacles to desire satisfaction such as locked cell doors or chains, but by his own desires. A drug addict lacks the freedom not to take the drug to which he is addicted. And he lacks this freedom not to take the drug because his own desire to take it, and not any external constraint, is forcing him to act. The addict is acting exactly as he desires to act. But despite the lack of any obstacle to acting as he desires, he is still not acting freely. He is still not free to act otherwise. And it is his very own desires that have taken that freedom away.

Our view of addiction shows that we naturally see being free – having a genuine control over how we act – as something quite different from merely doing what we want. Which is why we can happily deny that sharks, which have desires too and are often able to carry them out, are in control of their actions as we are.

Ordinary opinion also believes in a freedom specifically of the will. What we ordinarily believe about the will and its freedom is evident enough. It is exactly what the traditional will-based theory of human action implies. How we decide to act is up to us. It is our own free doing what we decide. Moreover our freedom of action very much depends on this freedom of decision. It is only because we can decide how to act, and it is up to us or within our control what we decide, that we have any control at all over our actions. Ordinary intuition very clearly makes our freedom of action depend on freedom of will. And it is this freedom of will that the addict lacks.

In the addict, we ordinarily think, freedom is lacking because the addict's voluntary actions are not determined by his own free decisions – by his own free will. The addict's voluntary actions and any decisions that precede them are instead being determined by his desires, by motivations outside his direct control. And as far as ordinary intuition is concerned, desires are quite different things from decisions. Unlike decisions, desires are passive occurrences, things that come over us without being directly our own doing. And that leaves desires as threats to our freedom, and not sources of it.

Hobbes and the tradition of thought that followed him has left us with a very clear, but also a very spare view of the world – a view which, in its totality, may seem rather alien to common sense, but which many philosophers still assume. The world is no more than a mass of material objects. And its history is no more than a series of events involving change or motion in these objects. These events will either be causally determined – or if the events are not causally determined then, by that very fact, they will simply be random to some degree. Actions are just another kind of event of this kind. For an action to occur is simply for prior events that are none of our doing – passive desires – to push us into motion. In the absence of a causal predetermination of our action by prior desires, there is room for nothing but randomness. Certainly, there is no room in this world picture for our ordinary libertarian conception of freedom. There is no room for freedom to be something that is exercised through a causally undetermined will, or something that can be removed by our own desires.

In the 18th century, the German philosopher Immanuel Kant accepted something like the Hobbesian picture of the world as a description of the world as we experience it – of the world as it appears to us. The world as we experience it is indeed a world of causally determined events. And action as we experience it is indeed nothing more than voluntary motions caused by appetites or desires. Since we have experience of nothing else, we have theoretical knowledge and understanding only of this Hobbesian world.

Kant though differed with Hobbes about freedom. In Kant's view, this experienced world did not suffice to provide anything recognizable as freedom. For Kant still believed in freedom as a freedom of will – a freedom that he conceived in fundamentally libertarian terms. And for Kant this libertarian freedom was still possible. It was still possible because the causally determined Hobbes world, the world as we experience it to be, is not the whole truth. The world as we experience it is not the world as it is like in itself. The world of experience may not reveal our freedom to us. But our freedom is still real, something that exists beyond appearances as a feature of the world as it is in itself apart from experience. So our freedom remains something in which we have to believe, and properly may believe. But freedom is still something of which we can have no direct experience, and no experience-based knowledge or understanding.

Has Kant surrendered too much? If we do believe in our possession of libertarian freedom, perhaps this belief may turn out really to be based on experience after all. Perhaps, and quite contrary to what Kant supposed, it is our own experience that reveals to us our capacity to take free decisions – decisions which are our own doing, and over which we have direct control. In which case the Hobbes world may be no more than a dogmatic fantasy, an imaginary creation that ruthlessly excludes much of what we directly experience about the world. So I shall eventually argue.

Freedom without voluntariness

Hobbes, we saw, denied that decisions are voluntary. We cannot take particular decisions to act at will, on the basis of prior decisions to take just those decisions. Precisely because decisions are not voluntary, Hobbes also denied that decisions are free. Since we cannot decide which particular decisions we will arrive at, we cannot control what we decide either. As far as Hobbes was concerned, freedom could come to no more than voluntariness. If anything cannot be done voluntarily, on the basis of a prior decision or desire to do it, it must be outside our control. It cannot be up to us whether we do it.

Our ordinary understanding of decisions is that they are indeed not voluntary. Common sense agrees that we cannot take particular decisions at will, or on the basis of deciding to take them. Nevertheless, common sense is profoundly convinced that decision-making is still free. It is up to us which decisions we take, so that we are free to decide otherwise. What we decide is within our control.

This shows that, though Hobbes may have identified freedom with voluntariness, we very clearly distinguish the two. The common-sense notion of freedom has nothing to do with freedom as the Hobbesian tradition understands it. Freedom, as common sense understands it, is quite different from any capacity to do things at will or voluntarily, on the basis of willing or deciding or wanting to do them. Things, such as our own decisions, can be up to us or within our control, without our having the capacity to do them at will. And this fundamental common-sense distinction between freedom and voluntariness is one with many implications – implications that I shall begin to explore in the next chapter, when I consider the attempts made by philosophers to do without freedom and, in particular, to make sense of morality without freedom.

Chapter 5
Morality without freedom?

Responsibility and self-determination

Ordinary moral thinking treats people as morally responsible for what they do or fail to do. Common sense takes moral obligation and moral responsibility to be for one's actions or omissions and their consequences. We can only be under an obligation to do things or refrain from doing them. We cannot be under an obligation for things to happen independently of our own doing, or be responsible for such independent happenings.

It is here that the idea of freedom becomes important. Why should it be for our actions or omissions that we are responsible? The natural thought, as we have seen, is that our actions and omissions are our responsibility because we can determine for ourselves which actions we perform. Our action is our responsibility – how we act can be our fault – because our action is something that we determine for ourselves. Central to ordinary thinking about moral responsibility is the idea of self-determination. And the most natural conception of self-determination is a conception of it as freedom. Our action is something that we determine for ourselves in so far as it is our action that we control if we control anything. Where action is concerned, we can be responsible because we ourselves can be in control.

Freedom and voluntariness

But freedom is not the only possible conception of self-determination. Many philosophers have been convinced that something else lies behind our moral responsibility. Moral responsibility, these philosophers agree, is certainly still for how we act. And this is indeed still because moral responsibility presupposes some capacity for self-determination – a capacity to determine things for ourselves which we exercise in and through how we act. But this self-determination, the philosophers allege, has nothing to do with freedom. It is instead entirely to do with something rather different. Self-determination is exercised as voluntariness.

As I have already explained, voluntariness is doing what one wants or has decided to do because one wants or has decided to do it. Now Hobbes, we have seen, wanted to define freedom in terms of voluntariness. One has control over an action if one has the capacity to do it or not as one wills or wants. But we have seen that this identification of freedom with voluntariness must be a mistake. For we think we have control over our decisions – that we are free to decide otherwise than as we actually do – although our decisions cannot be taken voluntarily. We cannot take decisions just on the basis of having decided to take them.

In fact, freedom and voluntariness really are very different things. Just consider the differences.

Freedom links the performance of an action to the alternative of refraining from it, and says that each alternative is available. To say that an action is performed through exercising freedom is to say that it was also up to the agent not to perform the action. So freedom is a single capacity that can equally well be exercised in one of two ways: to perform an action or to refrain from performing it. To possess that capacity of freedom or control with respect to an action's performance is, equally, to possess it with respect to the action's omission. On the other hand, nothing is said about how the performance of the action was caused.

Matters are quite the other way round with voluntariness. To say that an action is performed voluntarily is very much to say something about the action's cause: the action is done on the basis of wanting or deciding to do it. On the other hand, nothing whatsoever is said about any capacity to refrain from performing the action. If the agent also has a capacity voluntarily to refrain, that is a further and distinct capacity – one that might or might not be possessed as well. To use an example from the 17th-century English philosopher, John Locke: I can possess and be exercising a capacity to stay in my room on the basis of wanting to. I am staying in the room because that is exactly what I want to do. But, unbeknown to me, the door may also be locked. Even if I did want to leave, I would not be able to. I may be able to stay in the room voluntarily. But I cannot voluntarily leave.

Voluntariness can be used to provide an account of freedom – of its being up to us whether or not we perform a given action – then, only by appealing to an agent's possession of both of two distinct capacities for voluntariness: both a capacity to perform the action voluntarily and also the further and distinct capacity voluntarily to refrain from performing it. Freedom in Hobbesian terms must then amount, not to simple voluntariness alone, but to a special two-way voluntariness.

Not only does voluntariness look rather different from freedom. It even looks different enough to provide a distinctive and very different way of understanding self-determination – a genuine alternative to freedom when it comes to conceiving the self-determination that bases our moral responsibility. And that was how voluntariness was originally seen before Hobbes ever had the idea of linking the two, and of trying to explain freedom in terms of voluntariness. People who for one reason or other disbelieved in human freedom had already tried to explain our moral responsibility for our action on this different basis. Our actions were supposed to be our responsibility, not because we have any freedom to act otherwise, but because in acting as we do we are acting voluntarily. We are doing what we ourselves have wanted or decided to do.

Moral responsibility without freedom?

Voluntariness furnishes, after all, what looks very much like a form of self-determination. Surely if it is one's own decision or will that has determined what one does, one has determined one's own action for oneself. We find this notion of self-determination as voluntariness being appealed to at the time of the Reformation by John Calvin. We might not be free to act otherwise than as we do. But our actions can still be our responsibility because in them we are doing what we ourselves decide or will.

As a 16th-century Protestant Calvin took a gloomy view of human freedom. He argued that, thanks to Adam's disobedience and the resultant Fall and loss of Paradise, we are now trapped by original sin – and to such a degree that all moral freedom has been lost. We are predetermined to sin or do wrong by necessity, and lack any freedom to do right. As sinners, our actions are no longer within our control. Yet even in the absence of a freedom to do right, we can still be morally responsible for our inevitable wrongdoing because our wrongdoing is still self-determined in some sense. Our action may not be free. But it is still performed voluntarily, out of a genuine desire or will to do it:

> The chief point of this distinction, then, must be that man, as he was corrupted by the Fall, sinned willingly, not unwillingly or by compulsion; by the most eager inclination of his heart, not by forced compulsion; by the prompting of his own lust, not by compulsion from without. (p. 296) . . . he who sins of necessity sins no less voluntarily. (p. 317).

5. John Calvin, *c.*1550, French School

Nowadays there are a number of philosophers – the American philosopher Harry Frankfurt is one – who, like Calvin, want to detach our moral responsibility for how we act from any freedom to act otherwise. It is the voluntariness with which we act – the fact that in deliberately performing an action we are doing what we ourselves have decided or wanted to do – which makes us morally responsible. The freedom to act otherwise is irrelevant.

It is clear why some philosophers might want to base our moral responsibility on voluntariness rather than freedom. Voluntariness is easy to understand and make sense of. It involves no more than acting as we decide or want. Freedom is a far more controversial notion. To the extent that we naturally conceive of freedom in libertarian terms then, in the view of these philosophers, it really is very obscure what it could come to. It is unclear that there is any room for freedom thus conceived in a world where events are either causally determined or random – and where our actions are widely assumed to be no more than effects of our prior desires. Why not simply abandon the notion of freedom, and base our moral responsibility for our actions on voluntariness instead?

But there is a clear reason why common sense cannot give freedom up, and why voluntariness will not do as a substitute. For common sense believes that we are responsible not only for the actions we perform voluntarily, on the basis of having decided to perform them, but for our prior decisions to act as well. We think that what we decide to do is as much our intentional doing, as much our own action and so as much our responsibility, as what we subsequently do on the basis of our decisions. But, as we have already seen, decisions cannot be taken voluntarily. What we decide is not subject to our decision or will.

That we hold people directly responsible, not for what they merely desire, but for what they actually decide and intend – this is deeply part of common-sense morality. Recall the case of selfish Fred, who despite all that his mother has done for him is indifferent to his mother's good and intends only his own. We blame him, not just for failing to help his mother – concern for his own interests may in fact sometimes lead him to help – but for his selfishness. And this selfishness is not a mere feeling or urge that passively comes over Fred. This selfishness consists in the disposition of Fred's will – of his decision-making capacity. We blame Fred for deciding on and intending his own good alone – for never deciding to further his mother's interests as well as his own.

We can blame Fred for this because we regard what Fred decides and intends as his own direct doing – and just as much so as whether he ever performs the actions intended. Contrary to what Hobbes supposed, the will is not just a cause and motivator of actions, of the voluntary actions willed, but is a capacity for action itself. Which is why we hold people responsible for what purposes or goals they adopt or fail to, for what they decide on and intend. We think that the taking of a specific decision, the forming of a specific intention – which after all is the adoption by the agent of a particular aim or goal – can be something that the agent himself deliberately and intentionally does. Our decisions are not things that passively come over us, like a surge of desire, or the dawning of a realization. What we decide is itself our own intentional doing.

But since decisions cannot be taken voluntarily, since what we decide is not itself subject to the will, this has obvious implications for morality. It means that the kind of self-determination that ties moral responsibility to being for how we act, including how we decide, cannot be voluntariness. Perhaps it really must instead be freedom.

Chapter 6
Scepticism about libertarian freedom

Self-determination and libertarian freedom

It seems that self-determination, our capacity to determine for ourselves how we act, must take the form of freedom. And this freedom, its being up to us which actions we perform, cannot be the same as voluntariness. For there are actions we can control which we cannot perform voluntarily on the basis of deciding or wanting to perform them. These actions are the decisions of our own will.

But is freedom even possible? Our natural conception of freedom is incompatibilist, indeed libertarian. It is incompatibilist in that our control over how we act depends on our actions not being causally determined in advance by prior events outside our control. It is libertarian in that freedom so conditioned is believed by us to be a freedom that we can and actually do possess.

Compatibilism has historically taken the following view of freedom and the capacity for self-determination that it constitutes. According to Compatibilism, when we act freely, we do count as determining for ourselves how we act – but only vicariously or by proxy, as it were. What determines how we act is in fact not so much us, but things distinct from us: the various desires and other prior motivations that we happen to hold. These are desires that precede our own action as its causes – desires that fall outside our control as not themselves our doing.

Libertarianism, though, disagrees. Libertarianism says that when as free agents we determine how we act, it really must be we ourselves who do the determining. For our control over how we act to be real, it must come from us, and not from prior causes distinct from ourselves. As free agents, it is we ourselves, and not anything else, who must be the ultimate determinants of how we act. The question then is whether we really do have this capacity for independent self-determination. What would this demanding form of self-determination really involve?

I said at the very beginning that many philosophers doubt the very possibility of libertarian freedom. They suppose that freedom as libertarians conceive it – this capacity for independent self-determination – is impossible in principle. We saw earlier in very rough outline why. Now is the time to examine these criticisms of Libertarianism in more detail.

The randomness problem

One problem facing the libertarian has to do with the threat of randomness. By *randomness* I mean here the operation of mere chance. And randomness so understood, most people suppose, is quite opposed to freedom. If an event or process is developing at random or purely by chance, we cannot be exercising control over how it is developing. But – the critics allege – freedom conceived in libertarian terms threatens to come to nothing more than chance. For there really are only two alternatives. Either an action must be causally determined in advance – in which case the libertarian will deny that it really is free. Or to the extent that the action is causally undetermined, its occurrence must depend on simple chance. By banishing causal predetermination libertarianism has tried to make room for what it regards as genuine freedom. But in the absence of causal predetermination all we really find is chance – which does not amount to genuine freedom at all. I shall call this problem that libertarians face the *randomness problem*.

Of course, the problem is based on one key assumption. The assumption is that the only alternatives are these: either an event is causally determined to occur, or else its occurrence depends on mere chance. But surely belief in libertarian freedom seems to commit us to there being a third possibility – that there can be some events that are neither causally determined, nor merely chance, because they occur under our control, as an exercise of our freedom. Now it is clear that critics of Libertarianism want to exclude this as a genuine and third possibility. But it is not obvious why it should be excluded.

After all, what could be more plausible to suppose than this? Some events are already causally predetermined by prior occurrences and so are not controlled by us – they were bound to happen anyway. Then there are other things that depend on mere chance. As occurring by pure chance, these events also must be occurring without being controlled by us. These really are cases of genuine randomness. But other things are occurring under our control – in which case they are neither causally predetermined nor random. When these events happen more than mere chance is involved, precisely because the events are occurring under our control. Things are not just happening randomly. We are controlling whether and when they happen. Put like that, what could be more natural than to distinguish between these as three perfectly distinct and equally genuine possibilities?

Causally Predetermined	Causally Undetermined	Causally Undetermined
so	and	and
Uncontrolled	Uncontrolled	Controlled
	(Randomness or mere chance)	

To solve the randomness problem there is therefore one thing we shall need to understand: why should it have seemed such a problem in the first place? We shall need to understand why so many philosophers have taken it almost for granted that there is no third possibility – that causal predetermination or dependence on mere chance are the only possibilities that there are.

The exercise problem

There is yet another problem that faces the libertarian. Is libertarian freedom something we could ever exercise, in the only way that freedom ever can be exercised, through what we deliberately do, in genuine and intelligible action? The worry is that it is not – that libertarian freedom is at odds with anything recognizable as genuine action. Libertarian freedom seems to reduce what we do to no more than blind, undirected motion – to the equivalent of jerks and spasms. And freedom – genuine control – is not something that could ever be exercised through mere jerks and spasms. I shall call this problem the *exercise problem*. Let me now explain exactly how the exercise problem arises.

Freedom, remember, is something that we exercise in and through intentional action or omission. That is what our own action is: the medium in and through which we exercise our control of what happens.

But what is an action? Something done for a purpose, in order to attain some goal. Every genuine action has a purpose – something that makes the action intelligible as a deliberate doing, and that allows us to explain why the action was performed. Actions are not blind reflexes. Actions are always events that can be to some degree understood in terms of the goals of their agent. 'Why did you cross the road?', someone asks me. And if crossing the road was something that I really did intentionally do, if it was not something that happened through some external accident (a landslip pulled me across) or through a blind reflex (my legs went into spasm), there is always some answer. The answer comes from my purpose in crossing the road. Perhaps I am crossing the road just for its own sake. Or perhaps my goal is to get to the newsagent on the other side.

Indeed action and purposiveness, doing something as a means to a goal, even if only for its own sake – these seem to come to the very same thing. Not only do all actions have goals or purposes. Wherever we find purposiveness, we also find action. To do something in order to attain a goal, in order to fulfil a purpose, is always to be involved in *doing* – to be performing an action.

Where does the goal direction of our action come from? The Hobbesian view of action gives a simple answer. The purposes for which we act come from our prior desires – desires that cause us voluntarily to act in the way that we do. Take crossing the road. Suppose I am crossing the road in order to get to the newsagent. Then the following will be true. My legs will not be moving by chance, in some spasm, but as a result of a prior cause. And this prior cause will come, not from something external to me, such as a landslip, but from my own desires. I want to get to the newsagent – and to get to the newsagent by crossing the road. And that is why I am crossing the road.

My action counts as a genuine action by occurring, then, not through chance, or through some external cause, but as an effect of my desire to attain some goal by what I am doing. And the goal or purpose of my action comes from the 'object' of this motivating desire – from what it is that I desire to do. This story applies even when the action is being performed, the road is being crossed by me, just for its own sake. Here too my legs will not be moving by pure chance, but as a result of some cause. And the cause will again be a desire to attain some goal. In this case, though, the goal will not be a 'further' end or purpose. It will simply be the doing of what I do, namely crossing the road. Crossing the road is something that I want to do for its own sake.

For Hobbes then, action occurs only as a voluntary effect of prior desires. And it is from these prior causes – from desires and from the objects of these desires–that actions get their purpose, and so too their identity as genuine deliberate actions.

It follows that, on the Hobbesian theory, action is by its very nature an effect of prior occurrences outside our control. That is the only form that action can ever take. Actions count as such, and acquire the goal direction that is essential to action, only as effects of prior desires – desires that are passive occurrences that are not our doing, and so which we cannot control. In the absence of such causes nothing could count as an intelligible purposive action. It could be no more than a mere purposeless happening. And, as we have agreed, freedom, genuine control, can never be exercised through a mere purposeless happening.

The problem facing Libertarianism now becomes clear. Libertarianism says that free action cannot be causally determined by prior occurrences outside our control – such as by prior desires. But the Hobbesian theory of action that we are considering says that action only counts as an action at all if it is an effect of just such prior desires. And this detaches libertarian freedom from the very nature of action, and in a way that is deeply problematic.

Freedom is something that we are supposed to exercise in and through how we act, through our capacity for action. But on the Hobbesian theory, our capacity for action is identified with a kind of causal power. Our capacity for action is identified with a particular causal power of our desires, with their power to cause us to act as desired. That is what action comes to on the Hobbesian theory – managing to do what we want because we want to do it.

But far from ever exercising libertarian freedom through this causal power, libertarian freedom is something that this causal power actually threatens. After all, in libertarian terms we are unfree if this causal power comes in a strong enough form – if our desires causally determine our action in advance. The causal power of prior desires to influence what we do – this causal power which, on the Hobbesian theory, constitutes our very capacity for action – has to be limited if libertarian freedom is ever to be exercised.

It seems then that libertarian freedom is a kind of freedom that cannot be exercised through our capacity for action. Libertarian freedom is instead in conflict with, threatened by, that very capacity. But as a view of freedom, this is absurd. Any freedom that is genuinely possible for us – which is a freedom that we really could possess and exercise – must be exercisable through action. And so we have the exercise problem. Not only does Libertarianism appear to confuse freedom with randomness. It also seems to leave freedom something that we cannot exercise through how we act. But real freedom, any freedom that we could possibly enjoy, must be exercisable through how we act.

At this point some philosophers might wonder whether there really is a problem. They are willing to suppose, with Hobbes, that all actions need to occur as effects of prior causes, as effects of desires. But having supposed this, they insist that we then need to make a distinction. What takes away our freedom of action is not the prior causation of our actions as such, but their causal determination. Our freedom is removed, not just by prior causes, but by prior causes that actually determine that their effects must occur – that leave no chance that we will act other than as they cause us to. But surely causal influence can come in degrees. Some causes determine that their effects must and will occur. Perhaps other causes may be less powerful. They may merely influence whether their effects occur, without determining that those effects must occur. There may be causes that leave some chance of their effects not occurring.

Take smoking as a cause of cancer for example. Perhaps, in some cases, some people's smoking does causally determine that they get cancer. Given that they smoke, there is no chance of their escaping the disease. But we certainly do not know that this is ever true. It is perfectly possible that smoking often causes cancer, but without ever actually ensuring that the cancer arises. The smoking may markedly increase the chances of cancer arising; but it need not raise these chances to a certainty. There is still a chance that cancer will not result. Of course, the cancer may eventually be caused. But it will not have been determined.

Such causes that influence without determining are often called probabilistic causes. They merely give their effects some probability without actually ensuring that they occur. If we make this distinction between different kinds of cause, it will be argued, libertarian freedom can still turn out to be perfectly consistent with the Hobbesian view of action. What action requires is that it be an effect of prior desires. But these desires need not actually determine how we act. They may merely be influences on which action we perform. As causes, they may be probabilistic rather than determining.

However, this distinction between determining and probabilistic causes does not really help. The conflict between action and libertarian freedom is not so easily resolved. And it is fairly clear why. True, libertarian freedom is strictly consistent with actions having prior unfree causes, provided the influence of these causes is sufficiently weak, so that these causes merely influence how we act without actually determining what we do. But this causal influence, even if it does not actually remove libertarian freedom, is still a threat to it. Enough of an increase in this causal influence – the influence that is supposed to be exactly what makes an action our own deliberate doing – and you will remove libertarian freedom.

This means that if we add more of what makes action genuine action – if we increase the causal influence of prior desires – then freedom is ended. And this is surely intolerable. It is intolerable that what actually makes action action, and so constitutes it as the very medium for our exercise of freedom, should at the same time be freedom-threatening. It is intolerable that what gives action its very identity should have to be limited if freedom is to be at all possible. Freedom is something that we exercise through how we act. It therefore cannot be something that is threatened by the very nature of action.

So the problem is not that free actions cannot have causes. Even libertarians admit that free action can have causes, provided these prior causes are not action-determining. The problem instead is that if, as Hobbes supposed, being an effect of prior causes is what makes action action, action's very identity comes from a kind of causal influence that is freedom-threatening – that has to be limited for freedom to be possible. Libertarian freedom is left as something threatened by action's very nature. Such a threat to freedom is absurd. Freedom is something that our capacity for action allows us to exercise. So that same capacity cannot plausibly and by its very nature threaten and conflict with freedom.

The exercise problem looks serious. But like many problems it has more than one possible solution. We can solve the problem, of course, by abandoning the libertarian conception of freedom. We could follow Hobbes and identify freedom with a form of voluntariness, with the capacity to act as we desire or want. And this would certainly resolve the tension between freedom and action. Far from being in conflict, freedom and our capacity for action would be more or less identical. Both would be explained in terms of the same general capacity, the capacity for voluntariness.

But why abandon the libertarian conception of freedom? Why not abandon instead the Hobbesian conception of action that is causing it such trouble? After all, we have already seen that common sense does not limit action to voluntariness – to what we do, as an effect of prior motivations, such as on the basis of a prior desire to do it. Like the traditional will-based theory, common sense extends action to include some prior motivations themselves as well – the prior decisions and intention-formations on the basis of which we do many things voluntarily, such as crossing the road. These motivating decisions count as actions even though they are not themselves effects of decisions or desires to decide. In fact, as I shall argue, it is possible, at least in principle, that these decisions may even occur entirely uncaused – without being effects of anything at all.

It may then be that in decisions we find genuine action – genuine goal-directedness – but in a form entirely independent of prior causation. It may be that decisions count as genuine goal-directed actions, but without prior desires having to cause and push us into taking them. In which case the tension between libertarian freedom and action will disappear. The nature of action will no longer be explained in terms that threaten libertarian freedom.

The randomness and exercise problems compared

Opponents of Libertarianism say that it is an incoherent theory of freedom. But remember that there are really two distinct grounds for making this claim. Opponents of Libertarianism could have the randomness problem in mind. They could be alleging that Libertarianism turns freedom into nothing more than chance. Or they could have the exercise problem in mind. They could be alleging that libertarians are detaching the exercise of freedom from action. They could be claiming that libertarians are turning the exercise of freedom into something blind and unmotivated, by divorcing it from what makes what we do a genuinely purposive and intelligible action. These are two quite distinct accusations. They are accusations that would need to be answered in very different ways.

To reply to the allegation that Libertarianism confuses freedom with randomness, we would need to establish that libertarian freedom involves something more than mere chanciness – that it involves more than a mere lack of prior causal determination. To reply to the second accusation we would need to establish that there could be intelligible actions – genuinely goal-directed, deliberate doings – that were nevertheless uncaused. And, of course, we might manage to show one of these things without managing to establish the other. For example, we might be able to show that even entirely uncaused decisions could still be genuine goal-directed actions. But that would still leave open the possibility that as uncaused, or at least as causally undetermined, these decisions were being taken randomly – that as undetermined their occurrence involved nothing more than chance. We should still have to explain how what libertarians call freedom is more than simple chance.

The very possibility of libertarian freedom is under threat. There is the threat of the exercise problem. Libertarian freedom seems to be at war with the nature of the very action through which it should be exercised. And then there is the randomness problem. Libertarian freedom threatens to dissolve into mere chance. Or so it is alleged. It is very far from obvious how serious these criticisms really are. In the next two chapters I will try to resolve them – taking the exercise problem first, and then turning to the randomness problem.

Chapter 7
Self-determination and the will

Solving the exercise problem

These final two chapters will be defending Libertarianism. In them I shall try to answer the objections that have been made to the very possibility of libertarian freedom. This chapter will deal with the exercise problem.

The exercise problem is based, remember, on Hobbes's theory of action. Action is understood by Hobbes as a kind of effect – an effect of desires, and so of prior occurrences outside our control. So the causal power of these desires is supposed to constitute our capacity for action. But this same causal power of desires to determine what we do also threatens freedom as libertarians understand it. If this causal power is great enough, freedom is removed. The price of freedom, as libertarians conceive it, then, is the limitation of this causal power – the limitation, in other words, of what makes action genuine action. Hence the objection to Libertarianism: how can freedom, properly understood, ever be something threatened by the very nature of action? If our freedom is exercised through what we do, it cannot be something in conflict with our very capacity to do it. Libertarians must have misunderstood what freedom involves.

So the objection runs. To answer it we shall need to replace Hobbes's theory of action. And this is what this chapter aims to do:

to replace Hobbes's theory with new theory that is not only more friendly to Libertarianism, but which also gives a better account of action itself. The theory will be far more faithful to what we ordinarily believe, both about action and about the decision-making that so much action involves.

Action without voluntariness

Hobbes takes action to be a kind of effect – an effect of prior desires. Is there some alternative, non-Hobbesian way of understanding what action is, a way that allows actions to occur uncaused? There had better be, in my view. For we do naturally believe that action can occur in uncaused form. We allow for this possibility in the case of our own decisions.

Suppose that one afternoon, having paused to rest during a stroll, I decide to stand up to continue my walk, rather than stay sitting by the river or start to go home. This decision to continue my walk is my very own decision, a decision that I quite deliberately take. The decision then is my very own doing – an action of mine. But just because it is my own action the decision need not appear to be caused in any way. In particular, the decision need not appear to have been imposed or pushed on me by the causal influence of any prior desire.

Until the moment of that decision there need have been no detectable desire on my part whatsoever to go on with my walk. Prior to the decision there need have been no evidence or hint of a passion or other inclination that was somehow causing or impelling me to decide on that particular option. And that, I suspect, is precisely because there need have been no such prior desire. On the face of it, sometimes we can just decide to do things, without any desire or other passive motivation having pushed us so to decide.

What decisions we take and how we decide is indeed our own doing. A decision is not some passive event that comes over us like a feeling. That is something of which in everyday life we are deeply convinced. But this conviction certainly does not rest on any belief that we are caused to decide as we do by desires. Suppose I do just decide to do something, and it appears that I take that decision without any prior desire having caused me so to decide. At any rate there is no independent evidence of any such desire. Cannot my taking that particular decision still have been my own deliberate and intentional doing? Should the apparent lack of any desire pushing me into taking that or any decision lead me to doubt whether the decision really is my own doing – my own quite deliberately taken decision? A doubt so grounded seems absurd. The presence of such a desire seems quite inessential to my belief that my own decisions are indeed my very own doing. My own decisions are my own doing simply because they are decisions of mine – and not because of any prior causes they might have.

If this is right, decisions are made actions through being the kind of psychological events that they are in themselves, whether they are caused by desires or not. But how is this possible?

What does action involve? I have claimed that the one thing that it does involve, that does make it a genuine action, is purposiveness. To do things for a purpose, as a means to ends, is to be involved in action; and any genuine action is intelligible as something done for a purpose. So where does purposiveness come from?

In the case of actions that clearly are voluntary – actions that we clearly do perform on the basis of prior desires or decisions to perform them – this goal-directedness does seem to come from outside, from the prior motivations that have caused the action. It comes from objects of those prior motivations, from what those motivations are motivations to do. When I cross the road deliberately and intentionally, it is clear that I must be crossing on the basis of a prior desire or decision to cross. And it is equally clear that my goal or purpose in crossing must come from this same cause. It must come from the object of this same prior motivation, from what I wanted or intended to do in crossing the road.

But where decisions themselves are concerned, this is not so obviously true. When I decide to continue with my walk, that I take this decision seems obviously my own deliberate doing. And as such, the decision seems to be taken by me for one particular purpose at least. The decision is aimed at attaining one particular goal. When I decide to continue my walk, I have at least this purpose in so doing: that, as a result of this decision, I do continue my walk. That is exactly why we take decisions about which action to perform. We take such decisions to settle how we will act, by ensuring that we end up performing the action decided upon. My purpose in deciding to continue my walk is precisely to ensure that continuing my walk is what I end up doing.

This goal that my decision has does not appear to come from any prior cause at all. For example, it does not appear to come from any prior desire. Instead the goal comes from the decision's own nature. It comes from an object that the decision has as a motivation in its own right – from what the decision is a decision to do. The decision's goal is the performance of the very voluntary action that the decision motivates, and which the decision is a decision to perform. A decision's goal direction, the very goal direction that is fundamental to its character as an action, then, is internal to it. And this may be the key to understanding what action involves, and what makes an event, not a blind happening, but a genuine goal-directed action.

The practical reason-based model of action

At work is a quite different understanding of intentional action from Hobbes's voluntariness-based model. At work is what I shall call a *practical reason-based* theory of action.

We have seen that as humans we have a capacity for practical rationality. We are capable of deliberating or reasoning about which actions to perform, and then of deciding how to act on the basis of this reasoning. Perhaps action can be understood in terms of this capacity. Rather than understanding action in Hobbesian terms, as a voluntary effect of prior motivations, we can understand it in practical reason-based terms instead. On this new view, to perform an action is to exercise our rationality or our capacity for reason – but in a practical or action-constitutive way.

On this view, deciding to go for a walk counts as an intentional action, not because it is something that we do voluntarily, as an effect of a prior desire to do it – it is not – but because such a decision occurs as a special and distinctively practical exercise of our capacity for rationality.

What might make the taking of a decision an exercise of rationality that is practical or action-constitutive? Remember what decisions are like. In taking a decision to go for a walk I am exercising my capacity for reason. That is, in taking this decision I can be responding well or badly to reasons for acting as decided, and my decision can be appraised as sensible or silly accordingly. Now when I take a decision, this particular mode of exercising reason is practical or action-constitutive, I suggest, because it possesses what I have already argued is a distinctive feature of action. This distinctive feature of action is goal-directedness.

We can see how decisions are goal-directed when we consider what makes a decision a reasonable or rational one. If my decision to go for a walk is to be rational, then, first, going for a walk must indeed be a desirable thing to do. The rationality of deciding to do something always depends on the action decided upon actually being a good idea – a desirable thing to do. But that is not enough. Deciding to go for a walk must also be likely enough to ensure that I do actually go for a walk. This is why sensible, rational people don't take decisions about matters that their decisions clearly can't affect. Since the function of decisions is to lead to their fulfilment, that a decision has no chance of doing this is a conclusive argument against taking it. I may, quite rationally, want and hope to spend my old age doing useful and interesting things, rather than in idleness. But there is no point my now deciding to spend my old age being useful if that decision will have no effect – if, for example, given the long time yet to pass, no decision I took now would make any difference to my motivations in old age.

Contrast decisions with a rather different kind of motivation, a motivation that is intuitively passive, and which we do not ordinarily see as a self-determined action. Contrast decisions with mere desires or wants. Desires or wants certainly are not goal-directed in the same way. They are not formed with the purpose of ensuring that the object of the desire is attained – that what we desire comes true. And we can explain why desires differ from decisions in this way. For a desire or want to be rational, it is enough that its object – what is desired or wanted – actually be good or desirable. Provided that this condition is met, it does not matter whether the desire will actually make what is desired happen – whether the desire has any chance of making its object come true. Perhaps what we want to happen will happen, if it does, quite independently of the fact that we want it to happen – and we can be sure of that. Perhaps what I want is for England to win the cup, when I am under no illusions that my little wants, as a distant supporter, will have any effect on the outcome. That does not matter. If what I want really is desirable – if it really is a good thing to happen – it can on that basis alone be perfectly sensible for me to want it to happen. If at least from my point of view it would be very desirable for England to win the cup, England winning is something that I can quite sensibly very much want to occur.

Indeed, perfectly sensible people may not only want something to happen, but want it also to happen quite independently of their own wants. The very desirability of what they want might entirely depend on its happening other than because they want it to.

I might deeply want a grown-up son or daughter to do the right thing, but to do it autonomously, entirely on their own, because they have determined for themselves what they should do, and without my influencing them in any way. Suppose I fully expect and am quite sure that, whatever they end up doing, they certainly will do it autonomously: they will do it quite independently of me. That does not make it irrational for me still to want them to do the right thing. What, in those circumstances I cannot rationally do is decide that they will do the right thing.

That is because a decision is an action with a goal. A decision is an exercise of rationality that is directed at its object, the voluntary action decided upon, as a goal – a goal which that exercise of rationality is to attain or effect – and that makes a decision an intentional goal-directed action, an action whose rationality depends on the likelihood of its effecting that attainment. And in this case, where my child is concerned, I know that what I decide will have no effect on what my child will do. So deciding what my child will do would be pointless.

A decision is a motivation with an object. A decision is a decision to do something. But a decision is not an ordinary motivation. It is quite different from an ordinary desire. And that is because a decision's relation to its object is that of an action to its object. The decision is related to its object – to what the decision is a decision to do – as to a goal that the decision is supposed to attain. What shows this is not the fact that the decision has any particular cause, but something quite different. What proves the point is the way in which the rationality of a decision is determined – on the basis, not just of its object's desirability, but of the decision's chances of actually helping attain that object.

Desire is an object-directed motivation too – a desire is always a desire for something to happen. But desire is not practical in nature. A desire is directed at its object merely as something desirable, not as a goal to be attained thereby. So the rationality of simply wanting an event to occur does not depend on the desire's being able to cause that event to occur. I can want England to win the cup – and want this quite sensibly – even though I am sure what I want will have no effect on whether England actually wins. What I cannot sensibly do with this belief is decide that England will win the cup.

We have arrived at a model of intentional action that, as promised, is practical reason-based, and not voluntariness-based. The practical reason-based model characterizes intentional action, not as the voluntary effect of a prior desire, but as a practical exercise of reason. So one form that action can perfectly well take is the formation of a reason-responsive and reason-applying motivation – the taking of a decision to act. A decision may be non-voluntary. But a decision can still relate to its object, the action decided upon, practically, as a goal which, like any other action, the decision is being taken in order to attain.

We are no longer characterizing action as a kind of effect, but rather as a mode of exercising reason. What distinguishes action is not a special kind of cause, but a special kind of rationality.

Hobbes's theory of action says that all actions get their goals from without, from the contents of prior desires as passive motivational causes. Hobbes denies that actions ever obtain their goal direction internally, independently of prior causes. The Hobbesian view denies that actions ever have goal direction in their own right. Once we understand agency in practical reason-based terms, however, things become quite different. Deliberate action can now occur as a kind of non-voluntary motivation, as decisions to act that get their goal-direction internally, not from prior desires but from their very own objects. These inherently goal-directed actions of decision and intention-formation can then pass this goal direction on to the further voluntary actions that they motivate and explain. My decision to get to the newsagent motivates me to cross the road. And the decision's object and goal – that I get to the newsagent –

will then be shared by the voluntary action of road crossing which it motivates. And that means that at every stage the goal behind what I do can come, not from some passive desire that fate landed me with, but from my very own doing. The goal that I am pursuing is generated by my own decision to pursue it. I can be the free creator of my own aims and purposes.

The effect is to detach the goal direction of action from passive motivations such as desire. We no longer need appeal to prior desires to find objects or goals for our actions. The goals at which our actions are directed can be a simple function of what – freely and actively – we ourselves decide.

Traditional moral theory, as we saw, does view us as the free creators of our own goals or purposes. It regards us as morally responsible for our very goals and purposes, and not just for the outcomes that we manage voluntarily to produce. And common sense takes the same view – blaming people and holding them responsible simply for being selfish, simply for aiming at their own good and not at the good of others as well. The practical reason-based model of action backs this moral intuition up. It explains how our goals and purposes can be our own doing, and not just imposed on us by our desires.

We saw how great the impact of Hobbes proved to be. We saw that even Kant, fundamentally a libertarian in his view of freedom, retreated to the view that freedom and free action so understood is something of which we can have no theoretical knowledge. But notice that Kant still thought of action and its goal direction in traditional, pre-Hobbesian terms. According to Kant, our goals are freely adopted by us. Our goals are not imposed on us by 'nature', by the causal influence of passive motivations:

A *goal* is an *object* of free choice, the representation of which determines it to an action (by which the object is brought about). Every action, therefore, has its goal; and since no one can have a goal without *himself* making the object of his choice into a goal, to have any goal of action whatsoever is an act of *freedom* on the part of the acting subject, not an effect of *nature*.

Kant's position is really this. Free action involves the initial free adoption by us of a goal or aim; freedom at the point of the voluntary derives from this prior freedom of goal adoption, since it is through the free adoption of goals, through free decision-making, that 'the object' (the voluntary action aimed at and decided on) 'is brought about'.

The practical reason-based conception allows us to vindicate Kant's conception of free action. But the action by which we exercise our freedom need not be what Kant supposed it to be – something theoretically unknowable. There is nothing unknowable or metaphysically mysterious about action as conceived in practical reason-based terms. We are relying only on claims about action rationality that are evidently true, and common property to anyone with any understanding of what an action is. Actions are goal-directed events. And what makes them goal-directed events is that their rationality, whether they count as sensible or foolish, depends on some object in a way that makes that object a genuine goal of the action – something that the action is supposed to attain. An event is an action if it has an object, and if its rationality depends both on that object being desirable and on the object's being sufficiently likely to be attained through the event's occurrence. Decisions fit this model. So decisions are actions.

We have our solution to the exercise problem – a solution that preserves libertarian freedom as at least a coherent possibility. Thanks to the practical reason-based model, we are no longer characterizing action and its goal direction in terms that are inconsistent with libertarian freedom. Action is no longer constituted as such by some passive, freedom-threatening causal force that is not the agent's doing. The goals towards which an agent acts are no longer imposed on him passively from without, and in a

6. Immanuel Kant, 1791, by Dobler

way that therefore threatens his own freedom. These goals can instead be determined through the agent's own action – an action that can be entirely uncaused. Hence if, as Libertarianism supposes, freedom does depend on there being a limit to the causal influence of prior desires on how the agent acts, that in no way divorces freedom from deliberate action and what constitutes it. For the motivations that give our actions their intelligibility and end-direction, which thereby constitute our actions as plausible vehicles of our freedom, are no longer our desires, but are instead our very own decisions, which can occur as free actions in themselves. And it is from the freedom of these actions of self-motivation that the freedom of our action as a whole derives.

Believers in libertarian freedom of will are often criticized for being wildly unrealistic in their view of human nature. They are often accused of believing in some overheated fantasy of free agents as total self-creators – as responsible not only for their particular free actions, but for everything on which those free actions must depend. But that is not what I am claiming here. Our performance of any particular free action must, on any sane view, depend on our prior possession of the very capacity for free action. And this is a capacity that must be given, and that cannot be our own doing or our own responsibility. Nor need libertarians suppose otherwise.

This capacity for free action involves, in particular, a conceptual grasp or understanding of various possible goals – an understanding that, again, is a passive given, and that is not the free agent's own doing. It is only once this understanding of possible goals is in place that an agent's freedom can then begin. This freedom consists, at least immediately, in control over which of these possible goals the agent then aims at and intends – for example, over whether he decides to go on with a walk or, alternatively, to stay where he is.

It is action as the medium for exercising this freedom – action as constituting a decision to do one thing rather than another – which must and can be characterized without appeal to passive causation. If Libertarianism is to prove coherent, an agent must be able to decide for rather than against a given option without having to be caused so to decide by any prior desire for that option. The very identity of his action – the particular goal at which it is directed, what the decision is a decision to do – must not derive from a causal influence that, in libertarian terms, tends to remove his freedom to act otherwise. The identity of the action must be wholly the agent's own doing, wholly a function of how he exercises his capacity for agency, and not determined by some passive impulsion on the agent from without. This is surely the conception of human action and choice that libertarian freedom requires; and this is the conception that the practical reason-based model delivers.

Many modern philosophers write as if it were just obvious that all action is caused by desires, by prior motivations that are passive. But this is not obvious. Often, as when I spontaneously decide to continue my walk, the only ground we have for supposing that we are motivated to do something is that we actually have decided to do it. There need be no empirical evidence whatsoever that even before that decision there existed in us some prior desire that was already pushing or moving us towards doing that thing. That, nonetheless, we must have been moved into action by some such desire – this is an article of mere faith. And this is a faith that we need not adopt.

If this is right, decisions are made actions through being the kind of psychological events that they are in themselves, not by virtue of any prior causes that they may have. But notice that I do not deny that actions, including decisions, can, as a matter of contingent fact, be influenced by passive desires. If I decide to continue with my walk, it is certainly possible for me to have been caused to do so by, for example, some prior desire or yen to go on walking. My point is not to deny this possibility, but simply to urge that deciding to go on with the walk is not something dependent for its identity and nature on such a passive influence. Taking a decision to go on with my walk is something that, in principle at least, I can do without being influenced or caused to do so by some prior desire so to act. And if uncaused decisions can perfectly well be actions in their own right, there is nothing in the nature of goal-directed action that in any way constitutes a threat to libertarian freedom. The exercise problem – the problem of how libertarian freedom could be exercised in something recognizable as genuine action – this problem has been solved.

Chapter 8

Freedom and its place in nature

Is freedom a causal power?

The exercise problem may now have been solved. Action is no longer to be understood, in terms that threaten libertarian freedom, as an effect of passive desires. Action can perfectly well take uncaused form. Actions can occur as uncaused decisions, without being any the less genuine and deliberate actions. But the randomness problem still remains. Even though directed at definite goals, as uncaused or as causally undetermined our actions could still be merely chance performances. What intentions we formed could still be random and not an exercise of genuine control. We need to show that libertarians can distinguish causally undetermined freedom from the operation of mere chance; how by tying freedom to lack of determination by prior events libertarians are not at the same time equating it with randomness.

According to the sceptic, remember, libertarian freedom does come to no more than randomness. For there are only two alternatives. Either an action is causally predetermined – which libertarians insist would exclude freedom. Or, to the extent that its occurrence is not predetermined, it must be occurring by pure chance. In which case, the sceptic now insists, genuine freedom is again ruled out. There is no middle way.

I have already raised the question why should anyone suppose this. It could be that there is a third possibility – that, though causally undetermined, the event is not occurring by pure chance or randomly, and this because the event is occurring through the exercise of our freedom. Though causally undetermined, the event is not occurring by pure chance, because we are exercising control over whether it occurs. We need then to distinguish two kinds of causally undetermined event. There are those events that are causally undetermined and nothing more. These events are genuinely random in that their occurrence is dependent on mere chance. Obviously in the case of these events, any involvement of freedom in their occurrence is excluded. And then there are those events that are undetermined causally but still controlled. Here we do not have mere chance or randomness because something more is involved; and that something more is the exercise of freedom. The agent is controlling whether or not the event occurs.

In fact, there is a very important reason why someone might want to exclude this third and last possibility – that the event is causally undetermined but controlled. As we shall see, this last possibility is ruled out if we make one crucial assumption: that freedom, if it exists at all, must be a kind of causal power. And I think it has been precisely this assumption that has generated the randomness problem. So let me say something more about this assumption, about what it involves and why anyone should make it.

Clearly freedom – our capacity to control how we act – is a power of some kind. After all, freedom leaves how we act up to us. Freedom leaves, as one might put it, how we act 'within our power'. Our control of our actions is just that: an action- and event-determining power, a power that we have to determine how we will act.

Freedom, then, is a kind of power to determine events. It is a power to determine whether a given event occurs or whether it does not. It is a special power which, it appears, only rational beings such as we humans can possess, and which can be exercised only over and through action – through how we act. Freedom is a power to determine which actions we perform. The question arises then how this power relates to other powers in nature.

For there is another power to be found in wider nature – a power possessed not just by rational agents such as humans but even by inanimate objects such as sticks and stones. This power is causal power: the power to produce effects. And undoubtedly this power is importantly related to freedom. For freedom is a power that can certainly be extended through causation. Add causal power to some already existing freedom or control, and you get yet more control. Suppose I already control whether or not I perform a given action, such as whether I flick a switch. Then my control can extend even further through the causal power of this action, through its possible effects. Perhaps flicking the switch would cause the lights to go on or off. In which case, thanks to the action having this power to affect the lights, my control of whether I perform it also gives me control of whether the lights go on or off. The causal power of an action that I already control gives me yet more control – over everything which performing that action can affect.

It is tempting to suppose that the relation between freedom and causation could be even closer. Perhaps freedom is not only extended through causation. Perhaps freedom just is a kind of causation. In which case from the very outset the exercise of freedom consists in the production of effects. Any event over which we exercise control must occur as an effect that we have caused. Which means that there will really only be one event-determining power in the world, not two. There will simply be causal power, of which human freedom will be no more than a further instance.

We can see how satisfying this idea might be. It appeals to the profound need we have to simplify in our theorizing about the world. We want to explain as much as possible in terms of as little as possible. We want to reduce the apparently rich plethora of kinds of things and phenomena within the world down to the smallest possible range of fundamental elements – a simple and economical range of elements out of which the rich complicated whole can somehow be shown to be constructed. So why not replace what appear to be two distinct powers, freedom and causation, with only one more fundamental power, causation, of which freedom will turn out to be but a special case?

This option looks all the more attractive when we consider all the difficulties and doubts to which the very idea of freedom gives rise. What better way could there be to resolve these doubts and difficulties than by revealing freedom to be just the same familiar power as the power of stones to break windows, or the power of fire to boil water?

But if we do make this identification, the equation of lack of causal determination with a dependence on mere chance or randomness will follow. For mere chance or randomness just is sheer lack of causal determination. It is what you get from lack of causal determination and *nothing else* – including the absence of control. And if control is only ever exercised as a kind of causation – as a kind of causal power – then to the extent that events are causally undetermined, undetermined by any causal power, so to that same extent their occurrence will also be uncontrolled. And that does indeed leave their final occurrence, both causally undetermined and uncontrolled as it is, dependent on mere chance or randomness.

On the other hand, it really is not obvious that freedom is a kind of causal power. After all, sticks and stones do not possess freedom, though they or events involving them clearly can produce effects. Indeed most things that have causal power, which produce effects, lack control over how that power is exercised. A stone thrown at a window does not control whether or not it breaks the window. Once thrown against the window with a given force, there may be only one effect that it can have – that the glass shatters. Freedom is quite different. Freedom or control is inherently a power that can be exercised in more than one way – to determine either that a given action occurs or that it does not. We have control over which actions we perform, whereas ordinary causes lack control over which effects they produce.

On any view, to exercise freedom is to determine for oneself whether or not a given action occurs. Freedom is a power to determine. Many philosophers go further, though. They just assume that to determine and to determine causally must come to the same thing. In which case, on their view, what is causally undetermined would also have to be undetermined by us, and so outside our control. But this ignores the possibility that freedom might be a non-causal power; that in exercising freedom we might be determining how we act non-causally – and so in quite a different way from the way in which a stone determines that a window is broken.

There is a clear limit to the simplicity in nature. There must be fundamental distinctions, otherwise everything would be exactly the same – which very obviously is not the case. It is as important to do justice to the differences as to draw out the similarities. We do not usefully explain anything just by insisting, dogmatically, that things that are evidently different are really just one and the same thing. The power of freedom and causal power may provide a case in point. These two powers do look very different; and perhaps that is just because they really are distinct.

It is important to stress this point because the English-language tradition in philosophy has been so prone to neglect it. In the last 50 years, it has been particularly prone to ignore the point where things involving the mind and mentality are concerned. The mind, and especially the highly developed human mind, is clearly a remarkable and distinctive thing. In the mind we find things and phenomena that seem quite different from anything else in wider nature. We find consciousness, we find understanding, we find rationality or the capacity to respond to reasons – and we find freedom, the capacity to control the will and the further voluntary actions that depend on the decisions of our will. Or so we think. But rather than recognize and appreciate this distinctiveness, many philosophers have been immensely uncomfortable about it. They have taken the path first opened up by Thomas Hobbes – the path of naturalism, which tries to deny or abolish the evident differences between humanity and wider nature.

One option is that of naturalist *elimination*. This option is simply to deny that things such as consciousness, understanding, rationality, and freedom really exist. But the other, more subtle option is that of naturalist *reduction*. This option is to admit that each of consciousness, understanding, rationality, and freedom really does exist, but to make out that it is really nothing more than a special case of some other supposedly less problematic feature found more generally in wider nature. We try to characterize all that these things involve in other terms – terms borrowed from wider nature and not trivially equivalent to the phenomenon that we are trying to characterize. With freedom the claim will be this: that freedom is really nothing more than a kind of causal power.

Compatibilist naturalism and freedom as a causal power

Reductivist accounts of freedom as a kind of causal power have a native home. Their origins lie in the Hobbesian tradition. Compatibilists of this naturalist kind have been particularly keen to explain what freedom is in other terms and to view freedom as nothing more than a kind of causation. These compatibilists have claimed that freedom, the power we have over our actions, is a causal power of our desires. For they have assumed Hobbes's theory of action. They have assumed that to perform an action is just to do something voluntarily, on the basis of a prior desire to do it – this desire being an antecedent and entirely passive cause of how we act. In which case it becomes very appealing to reduce freedom, the power that we have over our actions, to no more than the causal power of our desires and appetites to lead us, marionette-like, successfully to do what they motivate us to do. Why should freedom not come to just this causal power? After all, on the Hobbesian theory of action the exercise of this very causal power is all that action involves. Action just is being led to do what we want by the fact that we want to do it. Unless our desires do produce such effects on what we do, action cannot occur at all – and so freedom cannot be exercised either. Any obstacle to the satisfaction of our desires just is, by its very nature, an obstacle to the exercise of freedom. So why not define the exercise of freedom as consisting, purely and simply, in such desires unobstructedly causing their satisfaction? Freedom just is the power of our desires to cause us to do as desired.

But this compatibilist reduction is quite unacceptable. It conflicts with the common-sense notion of an action which, as we have seen, does not define action in general as an effect of wants and desires. Goal-directed action can perfectly well take a form that need not be caused by desires or indeed by any other prior motivation. Goal-directed action can take the form of uncaused decisions to act. This means that we can no longer define freedom as a power of our desires to cause their satisfaction. For a block to the satisfaction of such desires need no longer be a freedom-threatening obstacle to our own action. What might prevent the satisfaction of our desires could be nothing other than our very own deliberate decision – such as, for example, our decision just not to perform the low action that all our desires and appetites are inclining and tempting us towards. The block to the satisfaction of our desires could lie in our very own deliberate action. We could be deliberately frustrating our desires by the contrary exercise of our own will. But if it is, not some external obstacle, but our very own deliberate action that is frustrating our desires, what would be inherently freedom-threatening about that?

Action, we now see, is not by nature an effect of our desires. It is instead something very different. Action is really a capacity deliberately to determine which, if any, of our desires are to be satisfied. And so our freedom, our control over how we exercise this capacity for action, is correspondingly a control over whether and which of our desires are to be satisfied. Our use of this power generally to frustrate our desires is not a loss of our freedom, but one possible way of exercising it.

Freedom, our power over our own action, cannot plausibly be identified as a causal power of prior desires or other passive motivations to determine how we act. And that is because we can deliberately use our own action, the very action through which we exercise our freedom, to frustrate our desires. If freedom is a causal power at all, it must be a causal power of a quite different kind.

Libertarianism and freedom as a causal power

Libertarians, of course, should never define freedom as a causal power of desires or other passive motivations to determine how we act. And there is a very obvious reason why. Since such a causal power is something that, in strong enough form, could perfectly well remove libertarian freedom, it and libertarian freedom must be quite distinct. For libertarians the causal power of any prior occurrence or happening over how we act is a potential threat to our freedom. So freedom can never be identified with such a causal power.

Yet many libertarians have worried that, if freedom is not some kind of causal power, there is nothing else for freedom to be. Action that was causally undetermined would not be determined or controlled in any other way. It would simply be action that was random. So these libertarians too have sought to identify libertarian freedom as a causal power – but as a causal power of a different kind.

There is only one other kind of causal power for our freedom to be. Not a causal power of any antecedent event or happening, not even that of a prior event or happening in our own minds such as a desire or feeling. Freedom must instead be a causal power attaching to and exercised directly by our own selves. Freedom must be a causal power, not of some prior action-influencing event in an agent's life, but of the agent himself. And, since freedom is inherently and essentially a two-way power, a power to do or to refrain, this causal power must be similarly exercisable in more than one way. The causal power that constitutes our freedom must be both a power to produce a given effect and to prevent its occurrence. And so we arrive at one very influential and popular theory of libertarian freedom: the theory that appeals to what philosophers term *agent-causation*. Freedom is supposed to be a special two-way causal power over actions, a causal power possessed and exercised, though, not by any unfree event but by free agents themselves. Freedom is supposed to be an *agent-causal* power.

Why should libertarians want to characterize freedom as an agent-causal power? Remember that the agent-causal theory is really doing two jobs. First, it is reducing freedom to another kind of power, revealing it to be but a special case of a phenomenon, causal power, found more widely throughout nature. So we have the satisfaction of locating even something so (supposedly) unnatural and exceptional as libertarian freedom as really just another part of nature. But secondly, the theory is also solving the randomness problem. If when we exercise freedom, we as agents causally determine how we act, then our libertarianly free action cannot be random. Free action cannot be random because it is causally determined – not by some prior freedom-threatening happening but by us ourselves as free agents. For one thing is clear and agreed on by everyone. Causal determination precludes all randomness in what is causally determined. The exercise of libertarian freedom is being very clearly distinguished, then, from randomness.

So when some action A occurs through an agent's exercise of his freedom, the agent himself is operating as a cause. Not any mere event or happening, not any desire or motivation, but the agent himself is causally determining whether or not he does A.

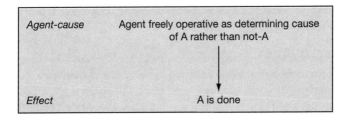

Agent-cause	Agent freely operative as determining cause of A rather than not-A
	↓
Effect	A is done

The occurrence of action A is not random, because it is causally determined. But its occurrence can still be an exercise of the agent's control because it is determined, not by an uncontrolled cause, but by the agent himself, as a freely operative cause.

It is of course important to this story that the agent's causal power must be exercised freely. The agent must control how he exercises his agent-causal power; he must control whether he causes or prevents A's doing. Otherwise, though causally determined by the agent himself, A's doing would be determined by a cause outside the agent's control, and libertarian control over whether A is done would be removed. But the claim that the agent controls his exercise of agent-causal power is anyway hard to deny. For that causal power is supposed to be nothing other than the agent's freedom; and how can freedom be exercised anything other than freely?

So should we view libertarian freedom as a form of causal power, as a causal power of agents? The issue is complex, and the arguments on both sides many. But there is an obvious consideration why we should not – which suggests that libertarian freedom cannot be any kind of causal power.

Remember that the agent-causal theory of freedom is supposed to do two jobs. It is supposed to give freedom a satisfactory location and identity within wider nature. It is supposed to reassure us that freedom is just another case of a very familiar kind of thing, causation. And it is supposed to resolve the randomness problem, by explaining how the exercise of libertarian freedom is distinct from randomness. I shall suggest that neither of these jobs is being done.

We do nothing to assuage worries about what libertarian freedom might come to, or to explain how it excludes pure chance, if we simply label it with another name – a name shared by a phenomenon that, in reality, is very different. That, I think, is all we are doing if we refer to libertarian freedom as a form of causal power. For freedom really is very different from causation.

As I have emphasized throughout this book, freedom, by its very nature, is a power that can be exercised in more than one way – which way being under our control. Freedom, by its very nature, leaves it up to us which actions we perform. But ordinary causal powers, powers to cause things, are not like this at all.

True, ordinary causal power can sometimes be exercised in more than one way. An ordinary cause may be fundamentally probabilistic. It may in fact be fundamentally chancy, not just whether it produces an effect at all, but which effect it produces. Perhaps, on the one hand, pushing that button will cause a light to turn green; or alternatively perhaps it will cause the same light to turn red. But even if that is true, that of course does not leave an ordinary cause in control of which effect it produces.

There is more. Such a merely probabilistic or chancy cause does not of course count as *determining* which of its two possible effects it produces, in the sense of removing any dependence of the outcome on simple chance. There is only one way for an ordinary cause so to determine the occurrence of one effect rather than another. It must be true that, given all the relevant circumstances and the cause, the occurrence of any alternative effect is left impossible. Should more than one effect be left possible, which effect the cause produces will be left random and undetermined – a matter of pure chance.

But when an agent determines what will happen by exercising

freedom, things are quite different. Suppose the agent has to choose whether to do A or not-A. And suppose that, given the circumstances and his presence as a free agent, either of A or not-A remains equally possible. Which action the agent performs need not be left random and undetermined. The power of freedom – his being in control – still allows it to be the agent who determines that he does A rather than not-A, so that which he finally does is not a matter of pure chance. But that surely implies that freedom is a quite different kind of power from causation. An ordinary cause determines its effects and excludes randomness only when its very presence leaves alternatives impossible. But a free agent determines his actions and excludes randomness in a quite different way. Why then suppose that way is causal too?

The consequence is obvious. Because the two powers, freedom and ordinary causation, work to determine outcomes and exclude randomness in very different ways, the fact that ordinary causal determination is randomness-excluding does nothing to explain how the exercise of freedom might also be randomness-excluding. You may label the power of freedom as 'causal' too, if you like, but attaching that label to it does nothing whatsoever to solve the randomness problem. For the labelling is merely that. It does not increase our understanding of how the exercise of freedom prevents the final outcome being a matter of pure chance.

Calling freedom 'causal power' does nothing to explain how freedom excludes randomness, or to assimilate freedom reassuringly to the familiar power had by sticks and stones. In fact, applying a common term to each, to both freedom and ordinary causation, only reminds us of the profound difference between these two kinds of power. So why insist on thinking of freedom as a causal power at all? Until and unless we are given compelling reason for thinking otherwise, we should suppose that freedom is not another case of causal power, but recognize it for what it is: a power of a quite new and different kind.

Libertarian freedom without reduction

We should conclude then that freedom is not a causal power. My initial exercise of control over my action, such as, for example, over a decision that I take, does not involve that action occurring as an effect, whether of my motivations or of myself as agent-cause.

But if freedom is not a causal power, what is the relation of a free agent to his free actions, the actions that he controls? It is clear what the relation must be. When I freely perform an action of the will – when I decide to go out rather than stay in – my decision is not an effect of me. And so it is not an effect of any power that I possess. My decision stands to my control or freedom, not as its effect, but as its medium or vehicle. I do not exercise my freedom to cause my decision. Rather my freedom is exercised in the taking of the decision itself. That decision is what immediately constitutes my exercise of my control.

Here is an analogy. Consider, for instance, my power as your creditor to release you from your debt to me. When I declare and say 'I release you', I do not exercise my power of debt-release to cause that declaration. For that declaration does not occur as an effect produced by my power to release you, but constitutes that power's very exercise. The declaration is the very medium in and through which the power is exercised. So too it is with action and the exercise of freedom. Action is the vehicle or medium for the exercise of freedom, not its effect.

Then it follows that libertarianly free actions really are causally undetermined. They may even lack causes altogether. But does this not land us back in the randomness problem? If the actions that the libertarian claims to be free are actions that lack any determining cause whatsoever, does that not leave them random? Are they not occurring by pure chance? No. Libertarianism is only in danger of turning freedom into randomness if – unwisely – it says that the exercise of freedom is *nothing more than* the occurrence of causally undetermined action. For randomness, as we have already noted, is what you get with causal undeterminedness and *nothing else.*

Libertarianly free action must, by its very nature, be action that is causally undetermined. And to that extent then, of course, such free action does involve chance. Prior to the agent's choice it must be causally undetermined, and so in this respect chancy, how the agent will exercise his freedom. But this is not inconsistent with freedom still being exercised. The exercise of genuine freedom is ruled out only if chance is all that there is – if an event is causally undetermined and nothing more, so that no power at all is being exercised to determine whether the event occurs.

But libertarianism has no business claiming that the exercise of freedom comes to nothing more than chance – to no more than the occurrence of causally undetermined action. For that is obviously false. All the libertarian should be claiming is that causal undeterminedness is a *condition* on the exercise of freedom. To read this incompatibilist condition on freedom as an exhaustive specification of all that freedom involves is quite gratuitous. It is to impose a reductionist interpretation on Libertarianism that is quite unwarranted. It is to read the libertarian as trying to do what Hobbesian compatibilists try to do – which is reductively to explain all that freedom is in other terms. There is no reason why the libertarian should be committed to doing any such thing.

The libertarian would be foolish to attempt such a reduction in any case. For it is inconsistent with a fundamental feature of common-sense morality. It is inconsistent with the moral significance that common sense gives to freedom in relation to moral responsibility. As we have seen, common sense appeals to freedom – to our control over how we act – to explain why it is for how we act that we are directly responsible, and not for our passive beliefs and desires. Common sense's explanation is contentful and intelligible. It is a substantial story why. The explanation is that we are directly responsible for our actions and not for our beliefs and desires because it is our actions that we control.

Any account of freedom that is to be consistent with our ordinary concept must permit this explanatory story to survive as, at least, a contentful explanatory story. Whether we believe the explanatory story given really is true or not, it must remain possible to give it. Why can we be directly responsible for our causally undetermined actions, and not for, say, causally undetermined desires? The obvious and immediate explanation is that we can directly control our actions, as we cannot directly control our desires, even our causally undetermined ones. But then for there to be anything to this explanation, there had better be more to freedom than the mere lack of causal determination in action. For otherwise all the explanation comes to is that we can be directly responsible for our causally undetermined actions and not for our undetermined desires, because our undetermined actions are actions. By reducing freedom to the mere lack of causal determination in action, what was an intelligible explanation of the restriction of moral responsibility to action would vanish into a clear non-explanation.

The same argument could be used against another familiar compatibilist reduction of freedom – this time not the reduction favoured by naturalist Compatibilism but the rather different one favoured by rationalist Compatibilism. This is the identification of freedom with practical reason. The rationalist tries to reduce freedom to nothing more than a capacity to act rationally. It should by now be obvious what is wrong with this reduction of freedom to something else. For we exercise reason, not only practically in how we act, but also non-practically in the formation, prior to our action, of passive beliefs and wants. And we can ask why, as rational beings, we can be directly responsible for actions and not for these passive beliefs and wants. The common-sense answer again appeals to freedom. We directly control those exercises of our rationality that constitute our actions, and not those that constitute our formation of beliefs and desires. But again, for this explanation to work, there had better be more to freedom than our capacity for rationality taking the form of action. Otherwise all we are left with is the thought that we are responsible for our actions because they are actions – which is no explanation at all.

And of course there is more to freedom than mere practical rationality, and we all know what it is: it is the distinctive up-to-us-ness of our actions, our being in control of them. And like so much else in our view of the mind, like being conscious, understanding something, being reasonable itself, we simply cannot adequately specify all that this control, all that this up-to-us-ness involves in other terms. Freedom is not simply a capacity to act undeterminedly. And it is not simply a capacity to act rationally. And freedom is not simply a kind of causal power. In fact freedom is not a causal power at all. As a power, freedom is simply what it is – and not another thing.

In defence of libertarian freedom

The sceptical case against the very coherence and possibility of libertarian freedom is far less formidable than it initially appeared. In fact, it now appears to be profoundly question-begging. And this becomes clear now we have uncovered where the roots of this scepticism really lie. They lie partly in a Hobbesian caricature of human action – a caricature that reduces action to nothing more than an effect imposed on us by our desires, and which brazenly excludes from human self-determination the very decision-making in and through which our self-determination is principally and initially exercised. And otherwise they lie in a dogmatic exclusion from the outset, both from the world and even from our very experience and understanding of the world, of the very freedom that is being denied.

The sceptical attack amounts simply to a dogmatic determination to describe the world only in terms that already exclude freedom as a distinctive feature of human life. The sceptic assumes that the world can contain no power other than causation; and that any event that is not causally determined by prior events must just be random. But if we insist on describing the world only in these terms, then of course it may well appear that libertarian freedom is not possible and cannot exist. But by what right do we so exclude such freedom from the very outset?

There is no convincing sceptical argument to show that libertarian freedom is impossible in principle – no argument to this conclusion that does not simply beg the question. But is there instead a convincing sceptical argument to show that even if libertarian freedom is possible, its actual possession and enjoyment is still unlikely? No. For example, no one has actually established the truth of causal determinism. Any causal influences on our action that can be traced back to our desires, and perhaps even further to environmental or genetic factors, seem in general to be merely that: influences. No one has shown that the generality of human decision and action is outright determined by such causes. Provided such causes do merely influence us without actually determining how we act, they leave room enough for freedom. Such influences may sometimes reduce or constrain our control over what we do. But they need not remove it entirely.

Do we have any direct evidence that we actually are libertarianly free? The sceptic will allege that we do not. The sceptic will allege that the only power that we ever directly experience is ordinary causal power – or its lack. And very plausibly, neither an experience of ordinary causation nor of its mere lack is enough for an experience of what libertarians understand as freedom. Of course, if the sceptic were right about this, we might well be left with, at best, the Kantian option. Our freedom would not be an object of experience at all, but something that we somehow just assume on other, perhaps more dubious grounds.

Yet by what right is it supposed that we do not have any direct experience or awareness of our own freedom? In fact, by a curious irony, just as the sceptic about freedom seeks to exclude any representation of it from our experience, so others have tried to do the same with regard to causation. Causation, of course, is the power that was earlier supposed by some, by compatibilists and agent-causationists, to explain what freedom is. Causation is the power that some philosophers hoped to use as a means to naturalizing freedom. If freedom could be made out to be a kind of causation, they hoped, then that would leave freedom a perfectly familiar part of wider nature. But one philosopher in particular – David Hume – tried to exclude causation, too, from our experience, and in just the same way that our sceptic wants to exclude freedom.

Hume thought causal power was just as hidden from us as the sceptic supposes libertarian freedom to be. He thought that our experience never actually represents causation to us. All we have direct experience or awareness of, Hume argued, is regularities in nature – one kind of thing, such as a fire being lit, regularly being followed by another kind of thing, water above it boiling. We never have direct awareness of something else, causal force, as a further feature in the world connecting these.

Such attempts to exclude from experience the representation of things such as freedom and causation are notoriously problematic. How far along this route do we want to go? We can soon reduce the content of visual experience, for example, to nothing more than the presentation of an array of differentially coloured surfaces. Surely it is obvious, the argument will go, that all we directly see are areas of colour. The rest, a world of solid material objects, is something which visual experience does not directly represent, but which we have to infer. Belief in a solid physical world is something going far beyond what experience itself ever reveals.

This is not an attractive view of experience. But how can it be resisted? I suspect that the only way is to appeal to the guidance that experience actually gives to our belief. If experience regularly and normally guides our beliefs about whether and when a given kind of thing is to be found, then experience must be representing that kind of thing and its condition to us. How else to determine what experience represents about the world, than by referring to its normal impact on our beliefs about what the world contains?

So experience regularly and normally leads us to believe in a world of solid objects, objects that exert and are subjected to various kinds of causal force. Experience leads us to believe in a world of objects such as sticks and stones – objects with the power to strike other objects and damage and destroy them. This then is the world that experience represents – not just a world of mere regularities unconnected by causation, still less just a world of coloured shapes.

Equally, experience regularly and normally guides us in forming beliefs about our freedom. It leads us to believe that we possess varying degrees of control over how we act – sometimes that this control is present, sometimes that it is diminished or even absent. Experience guides us to form beliefs not only about the causal powers of objects but about the non-causal power that is our own freedom. So freedom, as much as causation, is something that experience represents. And if experience is not an infallible guide in the case of freedom, nor is it infallible in its representation of causal power. But that does not show that freedom is unrepresented by experience, any more than it shows that causation is unrepresented by experience. If we still can acquire knowledge of causal power by relying on its fallible representation by experience, then we can just as well acquire knowledge of non-causal freedom too, and in the same way.

Arguing over the telephone with an awkward and deeply exasperating colleague, I raise my voice, deliberately speak ever more woundingly – and then, as my temper mounts, finish by quite intentionally delivering a gross insult and smashing down the phone. I feel myself doing all this – and I feel my control over what I do lessening progressively as I do it. I can feel myself just *losing it*. As I experience my action, I feel it is increasingly my anger that is determining how I am acting, not I. Who is to say that my experience of my agency is not representing all this to me? My experience is just the kind that leads those having it to believe that they are losing control. It is just the kind of experience that we would report as the 'feeling that one was losing it'.

We have a widely shared idea of freedom – a freedom or control of what we do that we naturally conceive in libertarian terms. It is an idea that is as much and vivid an element in our experience of ourselves and of the world as is the very different idea of causal power. So why try to turn one power into the other? And why be selectively sceptical of one power and not the other?

By contrast to causation, freedom seems limited to humans, or to at most humans and the higher animals. Freedom is unlike anything outside the mind in wider nature. But then the same is also true of many other features of the mind, such as our consciousness, our rationality and our very capacity to understand. Yet all these, having control of what we do, being conscious, understanding things, are aspects of ourselves of which we are directly aware – as aware as we ever are of anything. Human freedom is certainly as puzzling and distinctive a phenomenon as any other of these features of our mentality. But it seems no less worthy of our belief than any of these others – a belief that we in any case seem perfectly incapable of abandoning. We can as little lose our everyday conviction that much of our action is up to us to perform or not than we can abandon belief in our own capacity for reason or for understanding. And there is nothing yet to prove this conviction or the other beliefs accompanying it improbable or wrong.

References

Chapter 3

Susan Wolf, *Freedom within Reason* (Oxford University Press, 1990).

Chapter 4

Thomas Hobbes, *Of Liberty and Necessity*, in *British Moralists 1650–1800*, ed. D. D. Raphael (Hackett, 1991), vol. i, pp. 61–2.

Thomas Hobbes, *Leviathan*, ch. 12, ed. R. Tuck (Cambridge University press, 1991), p. 146.

Chapter 5

John Locke, *An Essay Concerning Human Understanding*, book 2, ch. 21, 'Of Power', §10, ed. P. H. Nidditch (Oxford University Press, 1975), p. 238.

John Calvin, *Institutes of the Christian Religion*, ed. J. T. McNeill and F. L. Battles (Westminster Press, 1960), vol. i.

Chapter 7

Immanuel Kant, *Metaphysics of Morals* (Ak. 6. 384–5; *Practical Philosophy*, Cambridge University Press, 1996, p. 516).

Further reading

The literature on the free will problem is enormous, and there is no possibility of providing anything like a comprehensive guide to it here. I have simply picked out a small number of representative works.

General

A useful collection of articles is *Free Will*, edited by Gary Watson (Oxford University Press, 1982; 2nd edn., 2003) in the Oxford Readings in Philosophy series.

The Oxford Handbook of Free Will, edited by Robert Kane (Oxford University Press, 2002) contains articles on every area of the contemporary debate.

For further reading on past theories of action from Plato and Aristotle onwards see Thomas Pink and Martin Stone (eds.), *The Will and Human Action: From Antiquity to the Present Day* (Routledge, 2003).

Ancient philosophy

Aristotle's *Nicomachean Ethics* contains a notable ancient discussion of action and moral responsibility. There are many modern English editions. Interesting modern discussions of Aristotle include *Necessity, Cause and Blame* by Richard Sorabji (Duckworth, 1980) and *Ethics with Aristotle* by Sarah Broadie (Oxford University Press, 1991).

Much of later Greek thought now survives in somewhat fragmentary form. A very useful collection with excerpts from ancient texts and some critical discussion is *The Hellenistic Philosophers*, edited by A. A. Long and D.N. Sedley (Cambridge University Press, 1987 – in two volumes, the first containing translations, the second containing original Greek texts). The collection covers problems to do with free will as well as many other areas of philosophy.

Along with Aristotle's *Ethics*, Stoic theories of action exercised a profound influence on medieval thought. They are discussed in Brad Inwood's *Ethics and Human Action in Early Stoicism* (Oxford University Press, 1985). A challenging but very interesting recent discussion of Stoic views of moral responsibility and freedom is *Determinism and Freedom in Stoic Philosophy* by Suzanne Bobzien (Oxford University Press, 1998).

One fundamental figure in late antiquity is St Augustine. His writings on freedom and the will are extensive, but their precise interpretation much disputed. A central text is *De Libero Arbitrio* (On Free Choice). This can be found in a recent English translation by Thomas Williams (Hackett, 1993).

Medieval and Renaissance philosophy

A central figure in the 13th century is Thomas Aquinas. One very important discussion by him of action and freedom is to be found in the *Summa Theologiae*, his overview of theology and of related areas in philosophy. This extensive work is divided into three parts, and the second part deals with humans as rational beings. This second part is further subdivided into two. The first of these, the *Prima Secundae*, contains in questions 6–17 an immensely interesting and detailed discussion of human action – a discussion that has been the object of much study and commentary ever since. This discussion can be read in a useful multivolume dual Latin and English text edition prepared in the 1960s by the Dominican Fathers (Aquinas's own teaching order). The relevant volume is 17, *The Psychology of Human Acts* edited by Thomas Gilby (Eyre & Spottiswoode, 1964).

Modern discussions of Aquinas on action include Ralph McInerny's *Aquinas on Action* (Catholic University of America Press, 1992), and *Right Practical Reason* by Daniel Westberg (Oxford University Press, 1994).

A key thinker of the 14th century is John Duns Scotus. A useful collection of his writings on the will and action, with critical discussion, is *Duns Scotus on the Will and Morality* by Allan Wolter (Catholic University of America Press, 1986).

For a detailed discussion of medieval theories and a comparison of them with Hobbes see my 'Suarez, Hobbes, and the Scholastic Tradition in Action Theory', in Pink and Stone (eds.), *The Will and Human Action*.

For Calvin's *Institutes of the Christian Religion* I have used the edition by McNeill and Battles in the Library of Christian Classics (Westminster Press, 1960). Those interested in Reformation disputes should also read the controversy between Luther and Erasmus, available under the title *Luther and Erasmus: Free Will and Salvation* edited by E. Gordon Rupp and P. S. Watson (SCM Press, 1969).

Hobbes, Hume, and Kant

Central to understanding Hobbes on free will is his debate with Bishop Bramhall, published in London in 1656 as *The Questions Concerning Liberty, Necessity and Chance*. Bramhall was the Anglican bishop of Derry, and shared an exile with Hobbes in Paris during the Civil Wars. In this debate Bramhall represented the will-based medieval scholastic tradition, and gave an account of human action and its freedom that owed much to thinkers such as Aquinas and Scotus. Hobbes's criticism was acerbic and deeply influential. I am working on a modern edition of *The Questions* for the new Clarendon edition of the works of Hobbes. Part of Hobbes's contribution to the debate exists separately under the title *Of Liberty and Necessity*. Excerpts from this work and from other of Hobbes's writings are to be found in *British Moralists 1650–1800*, edited by D. D. Raphael (Hackett, 1991). Worth reading is the discussion of action and the passions at the beginning of Hobbes's great political work *Leviathan* (see the beginning chapters, and especially chapter 6), edited by R. Tuck (Cambridge University Press, 1996). See also my paper on Hobbes and the medieval tradition mentioned above.

An account of action and freedom that is more complex than Hobbes's, but which clearly owes more than it admits to him, is to be found in book 2, chapter 21, 'Of power' in John Locke's *Essay concerning Human Understanding* – see the edition by P. H. Nidditch (Oxford University Press, 1975).

Modern English-language Compatibilism owes much to David Hume. An important statement of his views is to be found in *An Enquiry Concerning Human Understanding*, section 8, 'Of Liberty and Necessity' – see the edition by L. A. Selby-Bigge (Oxford University Press, 1975). Hume's scepticism regarding our knowledge and experience of causation is stated in the preceding section 7 of the *Enquiry* entitled 'Of the Idea of Necessary Connexion'. The interpretation of Hume on causation is disputed – see *The Sceptical Realism of David Hume* by John P. Wright (Manchester University Press, 1983) and Galen Strawson's *The Secret Connexion* (Oxford University Press, 1989).

Central to understanding Kant on action and freedom, and on morality generally, is his *Groundwork of a Metaphysics of Morals* (see, for example, the translation by H. J. Paton, Harper & Row, 1964). But Kant's views are complex and changed over time, even within his mature system. One useful discussion is Henry E. Allison's *Kant's Theory of Freedom* (Cambridge University Press, 1990).

The modern debate

There have been countless statements of Compatibilism within the modern English-language tradition. For a short paper, see A. J. Ayer's 'Freedom and Necessity', in the first edition of the Gary Watson collection on *Free Will* and in Ayer's *Philosophical Essays* (New York, 1954); and for a book, Daniel Dennett's *Elbow Room* (MIT Press, 1984).

A subtle argument around the place of blame and resentment in human life is Peter Strawson's 'Freedom and Resentment', in the Gary Watson collection.

Susan Wolf explores the rationalist view that free will and responsibility are to be identified with the capacity to act rationally in her *Freedom within Reason* (Oxford University Press, 1990).

For the sceptical position see Galen Strawson's 'The Impossibility of Moral Responsibility', in the Gary Watson collection, and also his *Freedom and Belief* (Oxford University Press, 1986).

Harry Frankfurt argues for basing moral responsibility on voluntariness rather than freedom in his 'Alternate Possibilities and Moral Responsibility', to be found in a collection of his papers *The Importance of What We Care About* (Cambridge University Press, 1988).

Further reading

A prominent recent defence of Libertarianism is Robert Kane's *The Significance of Free Will* (Oxford University Press, 1998). There is a good overview of recent libertarian theories in Randolph Clarke's *Libertarian Accounts of Free Will* (Oxford University Press, 2003). Both these books argue for positions rather different from my own.

My own views on freedom and action are developed further in my *The Ethics of Action: Action and Self-Determination* (Oxford University Press, forthcoming). A companion volume *The Ethics of Action: Action and Normativity*, will discuss the place of action within morality, and in particular the nature of moral obligation.

Index

A

action
  and freedom 5–6
  and purpose 17, 22–3, 83–4,
    95–103
  as practical exercise of
    reason 94–103
  as voluntariness 59–60
  without voluntariness
    92–4
addiction 68
agent-causation 111–15
animals
  actions of 22–3, 56–9
  and freedom 22–3, 66
  and reason 24–5
Aquinas, Thomas 29
Aristotle 3

B

belief 50–1
blame 8

C

Calvin, John 76–8
causal determinism 13
causal power 106
  and freedom 106–15
causes
  determining versus
    probabilifying 86–7,
    114
chance 15, 16–18, 81–3, 107–8,
  117

Compatibilism 18–19, 43–72
  naturalism and 44–5, 55–6,
    65–72, 109–10
  rationalism and 43–9,
    118–19
compulsion 10, 68

D

decisions 4–5, 25–42,
    92–103
  as actions 28–9, 94–103
  as free 4–5, 26–8
  as non-voluntary 60–4
  moral responsibility for
    36–7, 78–9
  uncaused 92–4
desires
  and compulsion 10, 68
  compared with decisions
    59–60, 96–8
determinism – *see* causal
  determinism

E

exercise problem 83–90,
    91–103
experience
  of causal power 120–2
  of freedom 67–71, 120–3

F

Frankfurt, Harry 78
freedom
  as an action-determining
    power 4–6, 105–6, 113–19
  as the basis of moral
    responsibility 7–12, 73–9

as distinct from chance 16,
    81–3, 116–19
as non-causal power
    116–19
as power to do otherwise
    1–3, 74–5
of will 4–7, 22–42
reductionist theories of
    109–19
whether experienced 67–71,
    120–3

G

goal-directedness – *see* action
    and purpose
God
  and human freedom
      38–42
  freedom of 49

H

Hobbes, Thomas 45, 55–72,
    99
Hume, David 11, 121

I

Incompatibilism 13–14, 16–18
indeterminism 15–20

K

Kant, Immanuel 70–1,
    99–100, 120

L

Libertarianism 13–14, 18,
    80–123
Locke, John 75

M

materialism 39–40, 56
moral responsibility 7–12,
    73–9

N

naturalism about freedom
    44
Newton, Isaac 14

P

political liberty 3–4
power 105–7
practical reason – *see* reason

Q

quantum physics 15

R

randomness
  as mere chance 16,
      81–2
randomness problem 81–3,
    104–19
rationalism about
    freedom 44–54,
    118–19
rationality – *see* reason
reason
  and the will 25–6
  as condition of freedom
      24–5, 45–6
  as preventing freedom
      49–50, 53
  practical versus theoretical
      50–1

whether identical with
freedom 45–59, 118–19
reductionism – *see* freedom,
reductionist theories of
responsibility – *see* moral
responsibility

S

Scepticism about freedom
18–20, 119–23
Scotus, John Duns 29
self-determination
as basis of moral
responsibility 8, 73
as freedom 9, 73
as voluntariness 75–9
Stoics 4, 14

V

voluntariness
as distinct from freedom 71–6
as possible basis of moral
responsibility 75–9
voluntary action 28–9

W

will
and action 6–7, 29–42,
92–103
and freedom 4–7, 22–42
whether immaterial 39–40
will-based theory of action
29–42
Wolf, Susan 48

Visit the
VERY SHORT
INTRODUCTIONS
Web site

www.oup.co.uk/vsi

➤ **Information** about all published titles

➤ News of **forthcoming books**

➤ **Extracts** from the books, including titles not yet published

➤ **Reviews** and views

➤ **Links** to other **web sites** and main OUP web page

➤ Information about **VSIs in translation**

➤ **Contact** the editors

➤ **Order** other **VSIs** on-line

PHILOSOPHY
A Very Short Introduction
Edward Craig

This lively and engaging book is the ideal introduction for anyone who has ever been puzzled by what philosophy is or what it is for.

Edward Craig argues that philosophy is not an activity from another planet: learning about it is just a matter of broadening and deepening what most of us do already. He shows that philosophy is no mere intellectual pastime: thinkers such as Plato, Buddhist writers, Descartes, Hobbes, Hume, Hegel, Darwin, Mill and de Beauvoir were responding to real needs and events – much of their work shapes our lives today, and many of their concerns are still ours.

'A vigorous and engaging introduction that speaks to the philosopher in everyone.'

John Cottingham, University of Reading

'addresses many of the central philosophical questions in an engaging and thought-provoking style ... Edward Craig is already famous as the editor of the best long work on philosophy (the Routledge Encyclopedia); now he deserves to become even better known as the author of one of the best short ones.'

Nigel Warburton, The Open University

www.oup.co.uk/isbn/0-19-285421-6